W9-ANA-588

NEW WRITING IN SOUTH CAROLINA

NEW WRITING
IN SOUTH CAROLINA

Edited by
WILLIAM PEDEN
and
GEORGE GARRETT

Published for the South Carolina Tricentennial Commission
by the
UNIVERSITY OF SOUTH CAROLINA PRESS
COLUMBIA, S.C.

CONTENTS

ix *Foreword*

xi *Introduction*

3 *The Just for the Unjust,* by DALE COLEMAN

26 *With the Red of the Fox,* by BETH PARRISH

32 *God Use Both Hand,* by CHALMERS S. MURRAY

39 *The Furnished Room,* by LYNN ROSMER

56 *Raghorn,* by COOPER A. SMITH

68 *Things that Vanish,* by ROGER PINCKNEY

73 *Adamus Perplexus,* by FRANK DURHAM

74 *Infallibility,* by FRANK DURHAM

75 *The Lamb,* by FRANK DURHAM

76 *Her Father Loved Horses,* by FRANK DURHAM

92 *Forests of the Night,* by GEORGE H. LYNN

97 *Tiger, Tiger,* by TOM PARKS

109 *The Man with the Cane,* by ROBERT JOHNSON

115 *Christmas Under Lake Murray,* by HELEN KING

121 *The Fish Collector,* by VERA KISTLER

130 *Susan's Tree,* by VERA KISTLER

131   *Billy Cocklebur,* by JOHN W. POLLARD

136   *Shower,* by FRANKLIN B. ASHLEY

137   *Three Cinquains,* by JOHN A. MITCHELL

138   *St. Simeon Stylites Comes Down,* by LUCAS CARPENTER

139   *Burnie Michelle,* by LUCAS CARPENTER

140   *The Wall,* by WENDY MATTOX

142   *One Day,* by PAMELA NAGLE

143   *The Poetry of Absolute Thought?,* by PAMELA NAGLE

144   *Beach Brawl,* by GRACE FREEMAN

145   *Cornfield,* by GRACE FREEMAN

146   *apricots,* by LEE S. MCADEN

148   *professor,* by LEE S. MCADEN

149   *Henry Small,* by WILLIAM E. MAHONEY

150   *Huckster,* by WILLIAM E. MAHONEY

151   *Return,* by BETTY R. FORD

153   *H.K.E.,* by JANE E. SMITH

154   *Short Ride by an Older Hitch-hiker,* by ROBERT HILL

155   *The Snow Came,* by ROBERT HILL

156   *Slow Thoughts on Quick Pictures: A Poem Interrupted,* by PAT KLEINHANS

159   *From Mouseketeers and Circus Boys to Monkees,* by KATHRYN BAIRD

160   *Hypocrisy,* by KATHRYN BAIRD

161 *With Apologies to Michael Caine, Dustin Hoffman and Sponsors of the Cannes Film Festival,* by KATHRYN BAIRD

162 *White Boy Speaks,* by HERMAN K. HARRIS

163 *The Pen: At the Jazz Festival . . . ,* by HERMAN K. HARRIS

165 *The Cham,* by GAY COTHRAN

167 *March, 1966,* by GAY COTHRAN

168 *They Repent for Mary Smith,* by GAY COTHRAN

169 *White Wind,* by ALOUISE D. COPE

170 *Movement,* by ALOUISE D. COPE

172 *Hattie's Rhythm,* by ALOUISE D. COPE

173 *Christmas Eve at the Hospital,* by LOUISE SELLERS

175 *To Edna Millay's "Tavern,"* by MARILYN MAHONEY

FOREWORD

Illuminating South Carolina's three hundred years of contributions to cultural development in an interesting way was part of the challenge to the state's Tricentennial Commission. Rekindling that fervent interest in the arts which was the hallmark of early South Carolinians was another. As part of this effort, the Commission's Creative Writing Committee set out to re-establish a community of writers within the state, and to do so within the context of the broader American literary scene.

This committee organized fiction and poetry workshops and conferences during the years 1968 and 1969; distinguished authors and lecturers were brought in to preside. Interest was generated through general media, and finally South Carolina's authors were invited to send in their manuscripts to be considered for this anthology. Established authors and unpublished writers contributed works which were read by a literary jury and by our two highly qualified editors. Their selections comprise this volume.

New Writing in South Carolina is a fascinating showcase of South Carolina writers. We hope you enjoy it.

JAMES M. BARNETT

Executive Director, South Carolina Tricentennial Commission

INTRODUCTION

Answering a student once, an eager and serious young man who wanted him to rate the "ten best American poets," W. H. Auden, wrinkling his already seamed face into a deep contour map of lofty bafflement, finally said, "My God, it isn't a *horse race,* you know."

He was quite right, of course. The arts are not a competition. All studying, scrutiny and self-scrutiny, strict criticism, and the largesse of great scholarship to the contrary, we do not know, in any final sense, how to offer more than the most tentative judgments. And we know that we do not know, no matter how we attempt to disguise our limitations and ignorance behind the authority of, say, a king's herald; though it is authority which is the proper uniform of all critics and editors, all *judges,* a uniform which must be donned though it is likely to provide as little comfort against rain or breezes as the celebrated new clothes of the fairy-tale emperor.

In a wonderful prefatory essay to *The Horse's Mouth* Joyce Cary tried to explain the nature of that singular human beast, the artist, whom he had drawn in the likeness of the unforgettable Gulley Jimson. One of the things he said of Gulley, and thus of all artists, is pertinent. "He is himself a creator, and has lived in creation all his life, and so he understands and continually reminds himself that in a world of everlasting creation there is no justice. The original artist who *counts* on understanding and reward is a fool."

It is all in the doing and the making, those moments when the artist is suddenly and truly the creator living in creation, that really matter. At such moments, all the living and the dead, known and unknown, join hands in equality. Then and there the difference between any poet or storyteller alive and Shakespeare or Homer or anyone else is a difference in degree and not in kind.

No, art is not a horse race, and that is the truth. But it is also true that the world of art is as fiercely competitive as any other, and that there is nothing new about this at all. Our oldest myths record the competitions of poets. The winners were rewarded and the losers were not allowed the luxury of self-pity or bitterness: Marysas, for example, upon losing a close competition with Apollo, was promptly skinned alive.

We begin by mentioning this because we have had many manuscripts to choose from, to judge. Our selections, here represented and in our best judgment representative, may or may not be the "best of the bulls." Within the limits of publication in a single volume, the choices here presented represent the best efforts of two different men, alike in their willingness to suspend, insofar as possible, such variable factors as fashion, "schools," and preconceived prejudices disguised as aesthetic authority. Each manuscript was judged first of all in terms of the standards of its own intent. Secondly, in a final winnowing, the surviving manuscripts were judged in a new context, the context created by the *idea* of this book, the relationship of each selection to the other and to the as yet unformed whole. Since, in essence, the submission of manuscripts for this volume was a competition, a jostling for small space, we could not permit ourselves, either, to stop to weigh and consider any of our selections against the invisible ghostly manuscripts of other fine South Carolina writers who, for one reason or another, did not choose to submit material. Their absence is regretted, but their decision is entirely their own affair. Their work exists outside of this volume but remains a part of the whole picture. Consider it elsewhere.

Similarly, we hope, you will have occasion to consider and to enjoy the work of the many others who did submit manuscripts but were not, here and now, chosen. Their work, though absent, is not irrelevant; for *all* who chose to offer work for this volume had a share in its creation by creating the context which made any choosing and selecting possible. And it should be remembered that by the same token all have a share in each poem or story in this book. Creation is a lonely vocation, in fact and by definition. A poem or a short story is written alone by one person and can be experienced by only one person at a time, no matter how many or how few may read it. But the act of creation takes place at one time (now) and in one place (South Carolina), a time and a place which possess their own artistic climate. That climate is, unlike the weather, the work of man; it is the product of all the living writers (each haunted by his private and public ghosts) of the time and place, whether they know it or not. We call it the *feeling* of a time and place. All the writers are involved, linked together invisibly. If any one should cease and desist at this moment, the feeling and the climate itself would be altered, subtly but palpably.

We need each other. This book, as it has developed, is an attempt to give some outward and visible sign of that inward and spiritual need. In that sense, it hopefully salutes not only the living and working creators here represented or absent, but the dead, known and unknown, who have shared in the making of the time and place. In that sense this book is an appropriate part of the celebration of South Carolina's past in the present.

Neither of the editors is in *fact* a South Carolinian. Yet both have deep roots there, going back to the earliest times. Both have kin, close or distant, who live there now. This seems appropriate also; for all presumed objectivity, we should nonetheless have some share in the feeling of time and place, part memory, mostly deeper than memory.

In our editorship we have, of course, been impressed by many things that seem to be happening or to have happened in South Carolina. None are exactly unique, being bound in kinship to the whole South and to the nation and, tenuously, to the events and feelings of the whole shrinking globe. The contributors to this volume clearly vary widely in age. Some are very young and their works bear the insignia of the student. Others are obviously older with memories and recollections that go back beyond the conscious imagination of the young. As one might expect in a volume representing the work of South Carolina writers, tradition coexists, easily or painfully, with change. Neither is the poorer for it. The old agrarian world is often summoned up in these selections, but chiefly in the past tense and often colored by nostalgia, a nostalgia which cannot be faulted, which is honest because it is not false.

In the poetry there is, as one might expect, an impulse toward formality and music, just as the prose is characterized by an inevitable earthiness, a sense of humor, a love of the eccentricities and energy of the spoken language. Yet most of the poems, minted in contemporary modes or carefully preserved in traditional forms, show full awareness of the literary currents and fashions of this age.

There is an intense consciousness of the great problems of the present, not the least of which is the conflict of the races. To the "outsider" who still claims kinship, the reactions of these writers are both interesting and reassuring. Black writers and the young tend toward anger and strong words, but anger is not the predominant mood. The predominant mood is one of honest self-scrutiny, of an attempt to understand or to correct; in the large sense, the overwhelming tone is one of compassion and charity. And charity never goes alone; faith and hope are also present, and perhaps more so than elsewhere, precisely because they have existed before. These writers seem to write out of courage, a courage which does not flinch from change.

In much the same way—and this, too, may be an unusual characteristic—the dominant mood is positive. The writers of this book do not shy away from plain truths and the ugly realities of life, human nature, and society. They are fully aware of the dangers and terrors of our times. What is special is their confidence and authority and courage. They see clearly and they see many of the same things as writers in other places, but they do not embrace the negative in the lust of despair. They believe in human possibility even as they often condemn the cruelties and follies they observe. Their courage is not worn with a swagger like a cape. It is natural, bred in the bone. All this speaks well for the future.

As to the future of letters in South Carolina . . . Here we avoid occasion for prophecy. All we can properly speak of is our impression of the present as we found it in the manuscripts considered for this volume. By current critical standards (which are all we have until they change or are changed) the work here is uneven. We would be less than candid to claim otherwise. All of them, we believe, are honorable and worthy in concept and execution; there is nothing here that is shoddy, sloppy, or shameful. Not all of them, of course, will please each reader, and not all of those that please will please equally; the same thing is true of any anthology. We should also point out that, for the most part, the material submitted for this collection was not the work of highly experienced, professional craftsmen. This, we believe, is a strength rather than a weakness. Most of the writers here represented, regardless of age, are *beginners*. Some have published more than others; some have a good deal more experience and skill than others. But there are none who cannot learn more craft, who are so fixed in habit and custom as to preclude the possibility of growth and change. Some will grow and change. They will be heard from again. That much is certain.

It is fitting that this anthology, published in celebration of three hundred years of history, should be . . . a book of beginnings. In that sense it is not a "definitive" collection, but is, instead, an experience of discovery. That discovery has been our pleasure. We relinquish it now, leaving it to the reader to have and to hold and, hopefully, to share with others.

NEW WRITING IN SOUTH CAROLINA

DALE DAVIS COLEMAN, born in Columbia, has lived in Charleston since 1941. She was editor and did much feature writing for a Myrtle Beach newspaper in 1959. "The Just for the Unjust" was first published in the College of Charleston's *Phoenix* by invitation of the editor in 1968. A member of the Charleston Artists Guild, she teaches at Sullivan's Island Elementary School. Mrs. Coleman is the wife of author Richard Coleman, who teaches classes in creative writing in Charleston for the University of South Carolina. The Colemans live and write on the Isle of Palms.

The Just for the Unjust

For it is better, if the will of God be so, that we suffer for well doing, than for evil doing. For Christ also hath once suffered for sins, the just for the unjust, that he might bring us to God, being put to death in the flesh, but quickened by the Spirit. 1 Peter 3: 17–18

Jasiel lay taut beneath the worn coverlet, his fingers holding the top of it tight under his neck. It was not yet light, but he could see the shadowy outlines of the lumbering chiffonier and the small desk and chair through the bars of the brass bedstead. In one corner of the room his brother Benjamin slept on a folding cot, his back hunched like a measuring worm, turned away from everything in the house. A lit-up Christ which their father had brought back from a trip to Mobile changed images through rippled plastic exposing a suffering, bloody Jesus whose eyes pleaded mercy, rolled toward heaven. A crack cut across it, made when it had once fallen from the wall. Jasiel turned his head to shut out the sight of it.

At their father's insistence, the door stood fully open, so that clean air could blow through and "run out anything bad that's hanging."

In a few hours they would all leave the old frame house that had been covered with paper brick a few years before and walk down the main street to the church. His father had done this each morning on his way to the Lord's work, but on Sunday he felt that it gave him more credit in heaven because his family came to heel behind him like the trail left by a shooting star. He liked to show them out. It made him feel like a whole man. A whole and holy man.

Today Mr. Justice would wear his black suit, and when he turned to nod to his followers along the way, his upper body would swivel at the waist and his great bull's head would tilt almost imperceptibly as though he was giving them permission to live in his world. He would find them on their porches, dressed for church, but delayed as though they were waiting for the word from some private vision. If there was some member missing his father would stop for a moment, his eyebrows meeting on the bridge of his nose, noting the absence to take up later, and then he would go on his way. His congregation did not always approve of Mr. Justice's gospel, and once in a while some of them fought with him for what they believed God had given *them* to see as His Word in their own, worn Bibles, but the look in their eyes most of the time showed a knowledge of Mr. Justice's hand of power in the town and an eroded belief that came from being worn out from fighting his tides.

As the Justices passed, each family would fall into the loose line behind them, so that by the time the preacher had come to his church almost the whole town reached far down the street behind him.

Each step of the church had a commandment cut into the stone risers. When their father judged that Jasiel or Benjamin had broken a commandment, they were sent to the church with a brush and a pail of water and scouring powder to wash, in full view of the town, the step upon which that commandment was written, as if to wash away the sins of the world, starting with their own.

The sudden bumping and demon screaming of air in the water pipes came down the narrow hallway that led to the bathroom and his mother and father's room. Benjamin cursed, tangled one arm in the covers and drew them over his head. Jasiel waited as he always did, hoping to hear the closing door when his father returned to his room, but it did not come. He closed his eyes tightly as he heard his mother's sleepy, protesting voice intermingled with his father's rumble. He could never hear what was said, though he wanted to, but always the woman's voice was abruptly stopped as though she had been cut off from everybody. Jasiel folded his arms tightly over his head and pressed the cold flesh of them against his ears to shut out the sounds of his father which followed her silence.

The colorlessness of predawn came through the window, finally, exposing the room slowly, as a print develops. Vague shapes, while remaining dimmed by the gray light, began to show detail. The oval mirror which hung on a large nail on the outside of the open closet door reflected the second image of the glowing Jesus, the pupils of his eyes rolled back almost completely under his plastic lids.

Benjamin moved restlessly on the cot with only his head showing like a dark ball against the pillow at the top of the mound of his body beneath the covers. He had been awake since Mr. Justice had violated the morning, and had, in his mind, gone through the books of the Bible, the twelfth multiplication table, a dirty song he had learned in school and all of the begats in the generations of Adam to shut out the sounds that came from the other room. Benjamin was fifteen, eight years older than Jasiel, and had chosen the cot when given his choice of a place to sleep when Jasiel was three. They had shared the bed until then, and suddenly Mr. Justice decided that it just wasn't healthy for them to sleep together.

Jasiel was suddenly aware of the exact space he occupied under this roof in proportion to the entire house and thought that it was not much room at all. One did not need much room to be alone.

He opened his eyes to see Benjamin sitting on the side of the cot, rising out of the shroud of sheets. He stood up without speaking or moving his eyes away from Jasiel. In this half-light, Benjamin, standing in his shorts, looked proportionately like Mr. Justice, although the boys had never seen their father any way except fully clothed right down to the wide black tie he always wore. Benjamin's vision moved down in a straight line from Jasiel's eyes until it met the floor and he turned to go to the narrow closet for his clothes.

A hanger, crossed with several others on the rack, sent them all falling in a tinny tattoo against a stored suitcase and to the floor when Benjamin reached for his suit. He leaned to pick them up and straightening, widened the door so that in the mirror he could see his brother, looking like an old martyr, waiting for an end to the torment, lying in the center of the bed.

"Good morning, poor in spirit," he said quietly. "You gonna get up?" He turned to go into the hall toward the bathroom.

Jasiel looked at the plastic face on the door. "Yes," he whispered. "There ain't nothing else to do."

His mother stood before the stove. She was fully dressed in a navy blue rayon dress with a light matching jacket, her strong thin fingers wound together in front of her as though they were holding her together. She was looking down into a pot of water boiling for coffee. Her face had the look of a freshly made bed, all in proper order like the lady in the cameo at her throat. Her shoulders straightened as Jasiel entered the kitchen, and she moved quietly to the sink and picked up the lean side meat to slice it for frying. Jasiel, meeting her there, reached up to the cabinet above for a glass and leaned slightly against her as he reached to turn on the water. Her expression did not change. She wore, always, the same face. Her washed-out eyes stared beyond any object to a point which only she could see, and when she had to have it, her mouth drew itself up into a transient smile, cold and humorless.

When Jasiel was five there had been a terrible scene about the raising of the boys. She was going to Birmingham to see her sister and she wanted to take them with her. Mr. Justice told her then that she no longer had the right to decide anything about them. "God give me boy children," he said. "A woman don't have no bidness with nothing except girls and babies. They only make for weakness after that. A proper woman is fixed to carry a baby and give her husband pleasure and see to his house. She ain't got nothing to do with the raising of children up to men."

After that she had kept herself inside the wall he built with the boys outside it. For a while Jasiel would go into a room where she was and stand near her chair hoping she would see him, but when she kept her face turned away as though he was a shadow of something she didn't want to remember, he withdrew from her little by little until finally he'd go and stand in the doorway to the room like he had lost something there. After a while he did not go at all.

When he leaned against her now, she looked at him quickly without raising her head, and then past him at Mr. Justice who filled the doorway ready for his breakfast.

His freshly pressed black suit was the uniform for Sunday and special things like weddings and funerals. His too-tight vest held the wide black tie that stretched up into a circle around his neck, knotted hugely at his Adam's apple.

He took them both in, then turned to go to the table which fit solidly, with just enough room for the chairs, in the narrow next room, swinging a black Bible at the end of his left arm. He seated himself at the farthest end of the table beneath the high, opaque windows which were circular, one large one flanked by two smaller ones that wheeled across the wall. His chair was the only one with a high, latticed back with serpentine arms which ended in round knobs over which he spread his great fingers and waited for his sons to sit down.

The smell of the meat frying followed him into the room, then Benjamin came in from the hallway just as Jasiel seated himself at the left side of his father. Mrs. Justice came in with a tray heavy with coffee, a pitcher of milk, and glasses. She set the coffee to the right of her husband's unopened Bible and straightened, looking at him.

"Good morning, Mr. Justice," she said.

Without looking up he opened the Bible, nodding slightly as though she was someone with whom he shared nothing. He waited until she was seated at the other end of the table, then rippled the upper corners of the huge Bible, seeking the text for the day's sermon. He thought of it as being a sort of holy brace to his family with which he hoped to give them a straight backbone for the walk to the church. It put them a little ahead of the others. His voice came down the table heavy with power like it was piped straight through from God.

When he finished reading the passage he slammed the Bible closed with a violence that made what he'd read seem even louder and looked at each member of his family to weigh his impact. Jasiel was watching the wild wheeling of the circular windows above his father's head.

The ritual road to the church seemed longer and more silent this morning. Following with Benjamin, Jasiel's thoughts were locked up

inside his head, slamming against each other looking for a way out of
there. Mr. Justice had not spoken to any of them since the reading of
the morning's text, and he glided along as though he was not touching
the ground at all. He gave the bits and pieces of his congregation permission to join him by looking straight ahead and frowning only
slightly.

When they reached the gate to the church they stopped to let Mr.
Justice mount the steps alone as he always did. He said that if the devil
was waiting anywhere he wanted to meet him headfirst and alone. He
walked forward, raising his arms up and out as if to gather what he saw
into them, then moved up onto the step of the first commandment and
turned to face the waiting crowd. Jasiel's eyes fell from his father's face
and he read,

THOU SHALT HAVE NO OTHER GODS BEFORE ME.

Mr. Justice wheeled away from them and continued to the top of
the steps where he grasped the brass handles of the doors and allowed
his worshippers into his church. They moved in silently, filling the
plain wooden pews which were old theater seats Mr. Justice had gotten
at a bargain from a renovated movie house in Birmingham. He liked
the fact that the seats were numbered. Nobody was allowed to sit
anywhere except in the seat which had been assigned by him. He found
the numbering system handy because he could look out and find his
target easily.

He mounted the steps to the tower and stood with his eyes focused
beyond all of them to the tall windows in the front of the building
which were covered with a diamond-patterned stick-on paper. The
family sat in the first row of seats so that they had to bend their heads
back to their shoulders in order to see him.

The pulpit was plain and painted white except for the gold letters
near the top which said

GOD MEANS BUSINESS.

He had it painted every few months and washed in between times. Mr.
Justice had ordered it made at a place in Mobile to suit a picture he
had long carried in his head, and paid for it with money made on

turkey shoots and chicken suppers. The man in Mobile who made it quit his job when the pulpit was finished. He spent hours with Mr. Justice trying to get that picture out of the preacher's head. He said when it was finished that he had meant to get it done if it killed him just in case it was God's business sent to him as Mr. Justice insisted, but that he could never again make another thing if it had to be built to specifications that were in somebody's head whether God put them there or not.

After nodding them into their seats, Mr. Justice summoned four men to come up for the collection baskets. He did not have any singing in his church. After taking the collection he set God right to work for him. Anyone who wanted to sing came on Wednesday nights to the basement of the church to a meeting conducted by Mrs. Justice called The Joyful Noise. The preacher never came to them.

"You pass the baskets and I'll pass the Word," he said, and the men began to move up the aisles, their eyes trying hard to remember what each member put in, knowing that the preacher might ask them later.

Jasiel tried hard to find some place to look besides at

GOD MEANS BUSINESS.

His mother sat submerged, cold and rigidly keeping spaces between herself and her sons. Jasiel looked at her. Her eyes had the look of a used, smoked-up glass chimney of a hurricane lamp, dull gray black and reflectionless. He looked around the room finding that same lifelessness until he came to seat 36 which belonged to Miss Dawkins.

Jasiel had been visiting her off and on since his mother had closed herself away from them. Nobody knew that he went there except Benjamin. It was something that Jasiel held as a special secret that he did not want violated.

Martha Dawkins was a large, warm woman who smelled of honey-suckle and onions. She took in sewing and anyone who would listen to her. She always seemed busy though not in the same way that his mother did. His mother went about her chores with a quiet tightness, straightening up things around the house in the same way that one who is left clears the grave site of their life, now dead, after years of dutifully tending it above ground. She woke up in the morning and went to bed at night wearing her weariness.

Miss Dawkins' house was in a never dwindling upheaval. Bits of cloth and thread and trimming everywhere made a patchwork picture of her rooms, although nobody ever knew whose sewing she did. Jasiel usually found her in the kitchen where something was always cooking, the smell seasoning every corner of the house. She was always glad to see him and started talking as soon as he was in view, all the while getting him something from the kitchen and launching them both into stories of Jesus and the prophets that left them running in and out of his head for days after his visits.

The edge of Mr. Justice's voice brought the boy back beneath the tower and straight in line for God's Business. "The Word was give into the hands of plain men," he said, "because there wasn't nobody else to handle it for God. The prophets was good, I guess, but they wasn't men and they was more than likely crazy from hanging around in the wilderness by theyself too much. When they did come out it made them talk all the time. People that talk too much ain't strong men. Strong men is silent and fights their way. A strong man has gotta keep his head going and his mouth shut and work his own will and be a man. And I been reading up on the saints. It looks to me like they give it all over too easy and that's why they all ended up dead—sliced up or grilled or stoned or with their heads cut off. I don't see no reason why no man with any kind of will of his own needs to let hisself be took away to no horrible death. A man holds hisself in and don't give a inch. Not to nobody."

Miss Dawkins shot up out of her seat, slamming it up in a folding position. The prophets were hers. Her eyes held Mr. Justice away from her, shutting him and his words in the tower as though she was avoiding a plague of devils. "False tongue!" she said. "A man opens hisself to God's will just like Jesus did. The prophets was His tools on this earth and they had sense enough to know it. They prowled the deserts and the woods and stayed away from such as you because they didn't want to be tainted by no false teachings but to keep pure for Him and their minds open to His voice. We ain't got no different God from what they had. When we listen He still speaks to us. Now you can fight against Him, because He give you the choice. Them prophets was burned up with loving Him and they didn't try to push Him around. It was *His* will that give them life every day. Not their own."

Nobody in the whole place moved while she made her way past all of the knees and left her empty seat facing Mr. Justice who stood with his Adam's apple swelling outside the noose of his black tie until it looked as though it would choke off every word he'd ever have to say again.

He lurched forward on the pulpit top and looked over his people for some sign that they might follow her. His family sat in silence, watching a vein in his temple throb, feeling that any movement might cause it to burst and spew out hell itself.

Mr. Justice picked up the black Bible and slammed it down on the pulpit. "Put on the whole armor of God, that ye may be able to stand against the wiles of the devil!" he screamed. "It's a terrible day when the heathen rise up and shout in the face of the Almighty. Go to your houses," he shouted, "Go and lock all the doors and pray to Jesus to wash all the bad thoughts out of your heads," he said, backing away and half stumbling down from the tower.

He went home bent, dodging in and out of the shadows of the greened-out oaks with the family following him. When they were in the house, he slammed into the bedroom. Mrs. Justice sat quietly on the sofa with her hands folded in her lap and the boys on each side of her and watched in the direction of the noises coming from the other side of the closed door. After a while she got up and went into the kitchen. At exactly one o'clock she had dinner on the table.

The bedroom door opened and Mr. Justice came out into the dining room where they were waiting. Deep lines tracked into his face like a tire tread, his eyes wild and glaring. He took his place at the head of the table and motioned for them to sit down, grasping the knife at the edge of his plate and straining forward.

"Proverbs 2:10–19," he said in a slow, precise rolling huskiness like lingering thunder. "When wisdom entereth into thine heart, and knowledge is pleasant unto thy soul; Discretion shall preserve thee, understanding shall keep thee: To deliver thee from the way of the evil man, from the man that speaketh froward things; Who leave the paths of uprightness, to walk in the ways of darkness; Who rejoice to do evil, and delight in the frowardness of the wicked; Whose ways are crooked, and they froward in their paths; To deliver thee from the strange woman, even from the stranger which flattereth her with words; Which forsaketh the guide of her youth, and forgetteth the covenant of her God. For her house inclineth unto death, and her paths unto the dead. None that go unto her return again, neither take they hold of the paths of life."

He grabbed at them with his eyes, trying to wring some understanding out of them. Only Jasiel's face held a question so Mr. Justice settled into the boy's look. "We been warned by God about the strange woman who lives outside His world," he said, surprised at the pleading tone of his own voice. "Way back in the beginning of the Word as it's give to us He's told us that they's danger in them women who live on the other side and stay behind closed doors and tempt men into joining them in their evil goin's on. There's been some that had to go see for theyself what was strange about them kind. What God said down along the years wasn't good enough. They had to know what them women was that was different from the sweet ladies they had of their own, and what it was those others had found outside of God's world. And even if we don't know how them men got caught into goin' there, we know what tempts men and always has."

The food in front of him looked like a stranger's meal. Nobody moved toward it. Mr. Justice slashed the air with the knife in his hand and brought it down hard into the table. "She don't know nothing about nothing!" he yelled. "The saints and the prophets was probable all crazy like I said, and Jesus didn't show he had no strength or a lick of sense. They ain't no power in the world can stop you if you set your own mind up for business. *He* could have set his mind on something besides the nails in his hands and feet and the blood in his eyes. He could have told straight out about God for a long time if he'd of showed a little guts and handled things sensible. But he just waited around for them to come and drag him off like somebody common just so's they could hammer him right straight through flesh and blood onto that cross. Now tell me that's smart!"

He threw himself back from the table, knocking over the chair, and went out of the house. Mrs. Justice and the boys sat for a moment, then got up and began clearing the table.

Mr. Justice rolled in combat with his demon pride all the rest of the afternoon. He kept seeing Miss Dawkins getting up and walking out of the church, and no matter how he tried to block it out, he saw the rest of the congregation following her, one by one, until he was standing there in his tower preaching to rows of numbered chairs. By nightfall, the vision of the empty seats mocked him as though he was being tried in a court where there was no judge or jury.

Just after dark he crossed the tracks and dodged through the willow branches in her front yard, trying to catch sight of her through the windows. He edged up quietly to the steps and knocked off a petunia planted in a tomato can on his way up, then jumped and stooped low until he was sure she hadn't heard.

Once he was up on the porch he could see her sitting on the sofa surrounded by pieces of scrap material which she was using to make a quilt that had a huge peacock in the center surrounded by purple and white triangles. She was sewing in a glaring peacock's eye. On the cushion next to her was an open picture album.

He watched her, wishing that he was anywhere else at all, but he had fixed his mind, and there was no going back on the decision to make her come back to the church and fill that chair. He knocked loudly on the screen door and smiled when he saw her jump at the sudden noise.

She squinted her eyes, trying to see who was there, then put aside the quilt and opened the door. "Evening, Preacher," she said. "Something to be done for you?" She held the door open for him to come in.

Mr. Justice did not mean to allow room for politeness. He crossed the room quickly and sat down in a blue flowered chair. "Seems to me there's something to be done for *you*," he said in a voice ground sharp by the afternoon's wheeling fear. "You didn't have no call to walk out on the Word of God like you done in front of all my people!"

Miss Dawkins took up the quilt again. A lapful of eyes made by the patchwork peacock pierced Mr. Justice's consciousness and he tried to stare back at all of them at once to keep from being caught off guard.

"God ain't never said no words like you was saying," she said quietly.

"Nobody ain't never walked out of my church," Mr. Justice said. "They ain't no other one, in the first place, so where else can you go to talk to Him? I don't want nobody getting no ideas, and I don't mean to preach to no empty room. God ain't willing for me to let a single soul get away so I got to forgive you. All you got to do is make a show of coming back and be sure they know how wrong you was. You got to come back and scrub a step when they'll be sure to see you. You got to clean up "Thou shalt not bear false witness against thy neighbor."

Miss Dawkins let her hand stray to the picture album on the cushion next to her and spread her fingers as if to protect something there from what he was saying. "Nothing you can say would make me come back," she said. "Somehow, Preacher, you left yourself open to the wrong voice and I hope to God you start hearing the right one. If you can't, I ain't listening to nothing else coming out of your mouth."

She stood up to show him to the door. Mr. Justice could not bring himself to believe that he had been unable to turn her decision, and a shadowy fear pushed the sight of those empty seats back into his head. He moved quickly across the room and stood close to her so she could see that his forehead was wet and his panic was steaming him.

"Now don't you trouble yourself none," he said in a voice she had never heard before. He reached out and slid his hand down her back until it was resting on the round of her hip. "I'm going to see that nobody bothers you no more. It's a hard and lonely place for a woman without nobody, but you ain't gotta put up with just any trash coming in here to you."

"It's time you went, Mr. Justice," she said, moving away from him. "The only trash I seen is what you come in here with and what you put in them poor people's heads. I ain't going to be nobody's trash can in *no way*. You take it somewhere else."

Mr. Justice looked like he was going to strangle on his anger. He was not used to opposition and she had moved away from him twice in one day. "Everbody in town's done seen them men coming here from other places. Just no-good strangers passing through—and they always come here. The devil sits on your bedpost and you're turning away God when he gives you a chance to make it right."

Miss Dawkins looked down at the picture album on the sofa. "Them men was friends of my husband. He used to have prayer meetings at the house and they come there to hear him. We had a boy nine years

old and a tractor run away with him when he was helping in the fields. He was throwed down in front of it and cut up when it hit the pasture fence. My husband got run over trying to catch it. Them men come here sometimes when they got to pass through and bring me vegetables and things knowing I ain't got nothing much to do with. Nobody knows it because it ain't nobody's business but mine and God's. I moved away from there because I didn't want no pity. Now you take your swill and throw it to them that's waiting for it. You won't have no trouble finding plenty of them, God knows. They ain't nothing that says I gotta listen to you here *or* there. I don't want the touch of your hands or the words out of your mouth."

Mr. Justice hadn't heard much of what she said. He saw himself in the pulpit preaching to a dark room full of pigs with red-lit eyes. He did not hear the frantic flapping of wings and the fearful flight of the chicken that he knocked off the front steps as he stumbled past.

Jasiel was lying awake, staring at the Justice Jesus on the wall when his father came home. The pleading eyes reminded him of what his father had said at the dinner table. He got up and went to the wall and stood before it, walking softly so that Benjamin would not awaken. He raised himself on tiptoe and looked straight into the plastic face. "If you was God, why did you have to beg for help?"

Jasiel went to Martha Dawkins the next morning. He stood on the sagging porch, looking past her into the room, gleaning and sifting his own arguments with himself—then reached for the screen door and walked past her.

Miss Dawkins watched him closely. "I just washed up some fresh picked berries that the chickens ain't got to," she said. "Come on in the kitchen and have some."

Jasiel followed her and sat at the round oak table watching her while she moved around the room fixing the blackberries and milk. She talked all over him, sheltering him with her chatter, knowing that Mr. Justice would take out his fury on the boy if he found out that Jasiel had come to her.

When she brought the berries and put them in front of him, Jasiel looked up quickly and grabbed her wrist. "How come Jesus didn't act

like no man and fight? How come He just give up like He did if He
was God? Mr. Justice said that if you just set your head to it you can
throw the power of God right at them. He says that God ain't always
right the first time even if He thinks he is. If He knows everything,
why did he make all them people and then decide He made a mistake
and get so mad that He drowned most everbody and started all over
again? Mr. Justice says that he guesses God does as good as He can,
but sometimes He says he's gonna do something and He don't do it or
else He messes around about it like all that arguing with Abraham
about burning up Sodom. If God didn't have no better sense than to
get Jesus in a fix like He did in the first place, then Jesus should of did
something sensible instead of hanging up there like he was deaf and
dumb and not using his God power to get hisself out of it. It looks
to me like a God with any mind at all wouldn't have ended up dead on
no cross. . . ."

Miss Dawkins let him hold her there, gripping her wrist until her
hand grew needled and then numb watching his child's face change to
a haunting, haggard old man's. "Jesus was born to die just like He did,"
she said quietly. "He wouldn't have done nothing to change a bit of it
no matter how hard the devil tried to meddle His mind with tempta-
tion. He knowed the exact time of his cross and when they was coming
for Him and what they was going to do. Being flesh and blood, God
come to earth as man, He didn't take to the pain of them nails, and for
a minute He asked His father to let Him out of it. But He left it up to
God, and it wasn't God's will and He knowed it. So He went with
them quiet and never said nothing. Sure, He coulda saved Himself, but
He wanted us to choose the hardest way to come to Him. It's easy to
love a summer day God. It's when He turns a cold and rainy face to us
that we got to learn to see through the pain and accept His will and
love Him because He lets you share in His agony. Jesus ain't no pretty
picture hanging up there. You gotta see Him on that dark hillside. And
when you see Him you gotta decide to hang up there with Him. Love
your papa, boy, but you got to be careful of a false prophet under your
own roof. We got to decide what it's right to follow."

Jasiel did not move, but seemed to be looking right through her to
that torn and tortured God staring through His own blood at him and

all the others he was dying for. The boy stood up quickly, his sight still fixed beyond her and his voice sounded as though it was coming through all of the clatter of confusion in his head. "God ain't got no right to be so mean and Jesus ain't got no right to be so stupid!"

He ran from the house pursued by the sight of that bloody body on the hillside and Mr. Justice in his black suit, still clutching the knife in his fist, chasing them both.

The next day Jasiel was to haul some bricks from a torn-down building to the church. The boys had worked for their own money in some way since they were five years old. Whether they got paid or not depended on Mr. Justice's line of preaching at the time. When he was supporting "man must make his own way" they usually got paid. But when Mr. Justice was endorsing charity, like as not he would look at his sons as though in holding back the money he was taking the Kingdom of God out of his pocket and giving it to them.

Mr. Justice had been doing his baptising in the river, but he noticed that business was falling off in the winter and wanted the bricks to build a baptismal pool at his church, feeling that salvation should not be seasonal. Jasiel got up before anyone else and left without any breakfast. He found a packing crate behind the feed store, tied a rope to it, and dragged it noisily down the street. He picked the dusty bricks from the ruins and filled the crate, but when he tried to drag it out to the sidewalk he found that he couldn't move it at all. He took half of the bricks out again and stacked them carefully so they would be easy to pick up again on the next trip. It was four blocks to the church, and he figured it would take him several days to haul enough of them for the pool. Mr. Justice had said that no man should profit except by the sweat of his brow and that Jesus was a common carpenter and not above working just like everybody else.

Jasiel worked until early afternoon. The sun was high soon in the day and the weight of the loads he was dragging soon pulled the muscles of his arms into knots of pain. It seemed to him that the sun wasn't ever going to stop, and when he began to feel dizzy from not having had any food, he decided to stop for the day. He left the packing crate in the basement of the church for safekeeping and began walking the railroad tracks instead of the downtown street home to keep from meeting Mr. Justice in case he was on his way to the church. He wondered if he would get paid for this job, and thought that if he had sure faith his father and God would be bound to let him profit by this sweat of his brow. Hauling bricks was just as good as sawing boards and nailing them.

When he reached the place where the railroad track met the road on which he lived, he stood looking first one way and then the other. He turned away from his house and headed instead for the small frame house set in the willows at the end of the road, passing several chickens who had made their searching way to the field next to the track. He knew that Miss Dawkins would be home no matter when he came.

Once he was under the cool, mantling green of the willows he could see the porch of the house which sagged on the side where the flower boxes were swarming with red, orange, and yellow nasturtiums. A green swing creaked softly on rusted chains in the breeze. The pealing paint gave the house a leprous look, but Jasiel thought that almost everything about Miss Dawkins looked like it was coming right to pieces except her love of God.

A radio was playing loudly in the house, and a preacher on a gospel program warned, "You cain't come to God unless you be born again."

Jasiel thought that if it wasn't one thing it was another and wondered how in the world he could be born again when he didn't know how or why it happened the first time.

The screen door stood slightly ajar and the front door was open. Jasiel went into the small, scrambled living room.

"They ain't no way in the world He'll take you, less you be born again in Jesus," the radio said, more loudly now.

Jasiel felt the willow-cooled air hit his damp skin, rubbed his hands slowly down the sides of his overalls, and with a swipe of his arm, smeared the dust on his face from one place to another. He did not hear anything in the kitchen, but he went on through to it anyway and out the back, loudly slamming the screen door and scattering a few chickens as he went. Miss Dawkins kept them for eggs which was a hardship on her because she hated chickens.

"I thank God for not making me no chicken," she said. "They don't never get a chance to stop pecking around for food and as soon as they plump theyself up to a good size, they get ate. The only thing worse than a chicken is them popeyed goldfishes that never give nobody no rest," she said. "They don't never go to sleep. Don't ever stop moving. They eyes is open constant."

Jasiel called for her near the henhouse but got no answer. He went back into the kitchen, scanned the cabinet tops quickly, and finding nothing but some cracked pecans, opened the oven.

"There ain't no way but to take Him in your heart," said the radio. "Don't let Him hang up there for nothing. They done all they could to Him. He never said a word. He let them curse him and spit in His face. He let them slash his body with whips and gouge His holy head with thorns."

There were cupcakes in the oven in a blue bowl. He took three of them and filled a glass with tap water. The blackberries floated in yellow skimmed-over milk on the table where he had left them the night before. Jasiel started into the living room wondering why, if Jesus was God, He didn't save Himself. "Looks to me like He ain't got much to say about hisself, much less anybody else," he said out loud. "It ain't no use praying to somebody like that to help you. He did fight some of them. He run them moneychangers out of the temple He was so mad at what they was doing. Maybe He just give up. He must of just got tired and quit."

When he reached the living room, he thought that he heard water running in the bathroom and decided that Miss Dawkins must be taking a bath. He fell back into the old wine-colored sofa, which was covered with soft-bristly stuff that tickled his palms when he ran his hand over it, and put two of the cakes on a paper fan that lay on the cushion next to him. He began to eat the other one.

The voice on the radio grew into a shuddering falsetto. "He layed down on the ground and let them hammer nails through His hands and feet, His pore body bleeding and the flies swarming in his open sores. On the cross He spoke a quiet word to His Father, looking for Him to give him some ease and some strength because nobody else could be with him. Down at his feet was those that loved him, but none that could be *with* Him. He could have split them haters open with a look of his eye. But He never did nothing. And then He went. The sky come all black and the ground shook under them and some among them knowed. But some didn't and before they give up His body they opened up His heart with a spear, just to make sure. They didn't see it was open before, and *that* was what He was trying to tell them."

Jasiel thought of the plastic Jesus with loathing. "If He didn't want to split them open with a look of his eye, why didn't He just float right on up to His Father from that cross?" he thought.

"They carried that poor broken body to that cold cave, and the others thought they was rid of Him. Jesus was a troublemaker. They didn't want nobody reminding them that they was sinning against God. Even the ones who knowed and loved Him best run like a pack of jackals and didn't recall nothing He said to them. For He named it to them when He said He'd rebuild that temple in three days and come up outta there and walk among them."

Jasiel had finished two cakes. He brushed the crumbs that dotted his front onto the floor, and still hearing the water running, took up the third one and went down the narrow hallway. There was water seeping from under the bathroom door, making a dark wet blot on the blue wool runner on the floor. He called out to her.

When there was no answer, he slowly tried the glass doorknob. The water covered the floor and still ran slowly from the tap. Miss Dawkins' red and blue polka dot dress was soaked and twisted around her like a wet banner. The water was flowing over the side of the tub into one of her shoes and onto her head which was twisted to one side and resting where it had struck the curved leg of the tub when she fell. Her eyes were staring unseeingly past her lumpy polka dot stomach at her right foot. One stocking moved slightly on the top of the water that flooded the floor.

Jasiel stood with his hand still on the doorknob, his mouth open to let pass the sound that would not loose itself from his throat though he was gasping and choking on it. His head jerked rapidly back and forth and his other hand closed tightly on the cupcake, squeezing it through his fingers. Then he felt the water running cold into his shoes and soaking his socks, and he backed slowly into the hall, closing the door quietly as though he did not want to disturb her. He backed all the way down the hall, then turned and ran through the living room and out of the front door, the voice of the radio preacher shouting him out.

The willow branches whipped at his face and caught his small flailing arms and shoulders. He fell at the railroad track on the loose gravel, but in one motion gathered himself up and didn't stop running until he burst into his mother's kitchen.

He threw himself at her, shoving her hard against the sink, pinning his thin arms behind her, the cupcake still sticky in his tight fist, his face rooting into her ribs. She was holding a bowl of freshly washed strawberries. They flew into the air in a red spray and rolled all over the kitchen.

"She's laying there dead!" he screamed in a dry, shrill child's terror. "Miss Dawkins is wet and dead!"

His mother sent Benjamin to the church to get Mr. Justice. She couldn't get Jasiel to tell her anything. Only faint, empty whimperings came from him and his small hands opened and closed on her thin arms as though he was trying to pump some life into them. It was the first time she had held him close to her in the two years since her husband had taken them from her. She took a wet, cool cloth and wiped some of the dirt from him and put him into his bed, hoping that he might sleep, but he lay with his eyes fixed on the plastic Jesus.

When Mr. Justice came in, they were still there, unmoving. He had gone to Miss Dawkins' propelled by his fury at the thought that Jasiel had gone to that house and the town was sure to find out about it. He came down the hallway to the bedroom, his expression cut into his face and his mind rehearsed. He stopped at the door and narrowed his look to include only Jasiel. The small face was swollen and fever-flushed.

Mrs. Justice did not turn in her chair. Her voice came flat and dry, but firm. "The boy is sick," she said.

Mr. Justice continued to hold his son in his glare, but his wife's tone cut away part of the speech he had intended. What he kept of it was on target. "Why didn't you turn off the water?" he said as he turned and left the doorway.

Jasiel's mother stayed with him looking out of the window and never touching him until his mind, unable to bear that wet, dead stare any longer, shut it out with sleep. During the night Benjamin woke up and

found him sitting straight up in bed, cold and silver blue from the
moonlight coming in the window, and fearing that his brother might
cry out and bring Mr. Justice, he left the cot and got into the bed and
took hold of the thin shoulders and pulled Jasiel down next to him. He
felt the small body trembling, and turning over on his side, tucked
Jasiel into the curve of his body. In a while the child quieted and fell
asleep.

Mr. Justice was at first resentful that the business of burying Miss
Dawkins fell to him. There was nobody else to do it. There would be
no church service. He decided that if she couldn't come into his church
while she was living, he wasn't going to let her in dead. But he was
suddenly caught with the idea that God had given him the burden of
praying this sinful woman into heaven—of seeing that He forgave her.
He walked around with this cross well-placed on his back the entire
day before the burial.

He chose the site himself at the back of the cemetery where a low
line of bricks marked the border of the lot. It had taken two days to
dig through the hard, dry clay. There had been no rain for two months
and the high mound of red clods circled the hole, making it even
deeper.

Mr. Justice got two Negroes to carry the pine coffin to the cemetery.
He walked just ahead of them in his black suit, turned almost blue by
the sunlight. His great head tilted down to his chest, his eyes on the
Bible in his hands. The hard heat brought streams of sweat down the
faces and arms of the Negroes, searing their backs through the faded
shirts, but a cloud bank was gathering behind the row of pines beyond
the cemetery.

Mr. Justice stood in the shade of the trees while the Negroes lowered
the box into the waiting grave, as though he wished himself removed
from the ugly necessities of the burial. When it was done, he motioned
them aside, stepped near the piled clay, and raised his head, the Bible
open in one spread hand.

His voice droned into the great hole of sky opened by the clearing.
"Lord, this was a woman who never knowed you. This was a woman
who lived a life that was hateful and prideful and who walked right

out of my church in front of everbody while I was rendering your Word. She give herself up to her lust and want and shut you out. She shut out all of us. She just took in them men who was strangers and then made up a story to suit herself. They *must* have give they-self up to the dark of her bed. What else could they have did there, Lord? You know why a man goes to a woman like that. A man don't go to a woman of secrets unless he goes for bad?"

For bad?

Mr. Justice stopped. The words backwashed him into the living room of a Miss Dawkins whose round, warm life he could feel heating his hand. He looked quickly down onto the top of the pine coffin. It seemed to him that he could see her staring up through the wood with mirror eyes in which he saw himself, tiny, knarled and naked, hunched on his own bedpost. He jerked his right hand up and quickly closed the Bible over it, burying it in the pages out of her sight. There was a swift threat of thunder, and he saw that the sky into which he had been firing his words was angry and slate-colored. His head was thrown back and a great drop of rain fell into his eye, blurring his sight. He looked accusingly at the Negroes who were watching him.

"It ain't nothing that can prove I was wrong!" he yelled across the grave at them. "Ain't I walked in his shoes and ain't you seen them all following after me like it says?" He held the Bible out in front of him with his hand still caught tight in the pages. He slid around in the wet-soft clay at the end of the open grave, pacing one or two steps in each direction. The rain, coming faster now, splotched and soaked his black suit. "Ain't that right? I led them out of the dark of their sins. I opened them up to Jesus and his Word. Didn't I do that?"

The Negroes had not changed expression. He saw that their eyes were used up, empty of response, and with a terrible dread of knowing Mr. Justice understood that he had seen eyes like them week after week as he stood before his congregation. He walked slowly around the hole and stopped in front of them, looking from one silent face to the other trying to force them to see him . . . to recognize him. As the last hope of that washed down their faces with the rain he knew that the minds of his people had been drowned in the flow of *his* word . . . not God's, and feeling that wave growing behind him, he turned, leaped over the mound of clay and began to run. The Negroes looked down where the Bible had fallen open on top of the coffin, it's pages splattering with red clay water, then took off through the trees.

The clearing was silent except for the rain. Jasiel came slowly out of the bushes where he had been watching the whole scene, his fist clutching a bunch of red and orange and yellow nasturtiums he had gathered from the window boxes of Miss Dawkins' porch. He walked quietly to the open grave and stood looking at the rivulets of muddy water running down into the hole in such an overfall that even the parched ground could not sponge it up fast enough. The rain slapped against his head, pasting his hair down almost into his eyes. The flower heads hung heavy with water in his hand.

He stepped up on the top of the slime of red mud. "Miss Dawkins," he whispered, "I fed the chickens and brought you some of the flowers from off the porch. I couldn't get in to see about the water because they went and locked all the doors." He leaned closer, trying to feel closer to her, and his foot skimmed down the side of the hill of wet clay.

He fell face down on the coffin lid, one leg wedged between the box and the grave wall. The flowers fell around him, floating on the muddy water that was rising around the coffin, their faces drowned. The pain in his leg was terrible and the fall knocked the breath out of him, but he forced himself up, clawing at the slick wall of mud, his small hands searching for something with which to pull himself out. The rain lashed his tight, frightened face that was twisting with a growing moan. The ropes with which the Negroes had lowered the coffin snaked up over the mound but he could not use them. He finally found the end of a root runner about halfway up the mud wall and grabbed it, but there were no footholds and nothing to grasp at the top, and he fell back onto the coffin. The pain in his leg ran up through him like an electric shock.

He lay spread over the wooden box and began beating it with his fists. "You ain't gonna rise up no more than nobody else did!" he screamed. "You ain't gonna git up outta there and all of them saints and prophets and Jesus hisself ain't gonna help you no more than they helped theyself. Why don't nobody do nothing? You'll just lay there in that muddy water and let them come and throw dirt in your face the same as he did. An' you won't never say a word because you *cain't!*"

The rain muted the sound of his crying. He pushed his small, narrow body hard against the wood of the coffin trying to press through it into her. "Why do you have to leave me? They ain't gonna put me in no box and sink me in no slime! Never! And you ain't gonna be born again and I wouldn't know you if you was because they ain't no such thing and he is dead the same as you. Your eyes was staring and your face was all blue and cold just like his. Get up, Miss Dawkins! Get up and help me! You ain't going to God. You're leaving me!"

The hardness of the pain in his leg intensified everything else and he could feel the sting of each raindrop on his back. The coolness of the air seemed to open his head, to make a space in his delirium, wiping out the heat of the fever. He tried to push himself up on his knees but managed only to raise his head slightly. "O God! I *know* where them eyes of Jesus was looking," he moaned. "They was looking past everything and everybody right back in his own head . . . inside hisself . . . at you. At your cold and rainy face right through his pain like Miss Dawkins said."

He tried to focus his sight on a yellow flower that was sinking in the water. "I'm trying to see you God, and I hope you can see me. Nobody will come in this rain and find me. Please come and find me. You don't mind the rain." He slumped forward, unconscious.

After the downpour, the Negroes, coming back to fill the grave, found that the water had caved in the sides of it, covering the coffin. They saw the flower, bright red and mired in the mud at the edge of the hole, and the ends of Jasiel's fingers, barely showing.

BETH CRAWFORD PARRISH grew up in Columbia. When she was nineteen, her one-act play was produced at Agnes Scott College and won a Southern Literary Festival prize. The story in this anthology was first written when she was a junior at Agnes Scott College. It has since been revised many times. Mrs. Parrish lives in New Jersey with her husband, an engineer, and their three children. She is currently working on a short story and a book for children.

With the Red of the Fox

Red flashes spaced by thin pines came faster. The fox rushed insurgently on a line that became unbroken for Mary's eyes. The fox was one long sweep of red-brushed tail wired to a tightly muscled body.

Mary leaned with him from where she stood, not sixty feet away, braced solidly against the chicken coop. She stood like that, weight over her toes, sucking air into her mouth and feeling her nostrils pull downward to breathe the pure freedom that she imagined swept from his movement backward to her.

"Devil! Steal my chickens, red devil? I'll air your hide with buckshot," she called after him, a smile pulling tight the lines around her mouth. "You'd make a beautiful collar, fine feller, for some fancy woman to tack on her coat. Run, red 'un!"

No longer aware of the wire fence printing red circles on her bare legs, Mary thought only of the bright fur, now surging straight, now curving smoothly.

When the wind changed, Mary noticed that the sun had blinked off below the gray line of swamp beyond which she could not see. Her hair began to whip across her face. The wind tossed it into her mouth. The gray hair, like threads of a web, caught on her forehead and over her eyes. The heat of the fox had gone and her fading hair mocked a desire to spring after him.

Robert, her husband, would be lying in wait for his supper. Mary clicked to the gate of the chicken yard and walked to the narrow white frame house. Robert was in bed straining to hear the whine of the back screen door. He was sixteen years older than Mary, and he was gradually dying. His face looked like the wrinkled inside of a dried mushroom. He clung with his long hands to the sheets as if this effort gave him comfort, occasionally letting the fingers of one hand creep down the side of the bed to the square muzzle of Votan, his mongrel dog. Votan was long and narrow like a coffin and just as angular. Recently most of his hair had fallen out so that pink patches with specks of black fungus on them appeared over the ridge of his back.

"Milk fo' dinner." Robert called Mary before she could sweep the dog hairs from the kitchen floor.

"In a minute, Robert. I'm comin' soon as I can clean up that hound's moltings."

"Hound what? Hound's . . . ?" Robert swallowed the last word heavily in his throat. "He's too old for you, ain't that right? Ya hear? You'd like to shoot him and be done with it." The old man curved his bony neck back over the pillow to rest from the strain of his words.

"He's a burdensome, filthy, lazy cur." Her voice lowered as she reached the last words. "I'm coming with your milk."

Mary lifted his rounded shoulders and guided the glass to his mouth. Robert jerked away from the glass after one sip. "Sour." His mouth squirmed. He stuck his head back over the glass and spit out a mouthful of milk. "Trying to kill me with filth?" He fell back weakly.

"I hope you can eat the soup I made." Mary said listlessly. "You probably won't like it." She wiped the outside of the glass on her apron, stumbled against Votan, and went back to the kitchen.

Mary could sense a storm approaching. The kitchen windowpane rattled occasionally and the scrub oak that stood against the house was rubbing its branches over the gutters and, with a rough jerk, down the shingles of the roof.

"Feed Votan!" Robert strained his voice upward to reach her. "Starvin' him? Are ya?" He questioned. Mary poured the milk from Robert's glass into a cracked yellow cereal bowl on the floor. She stirred some bran into the milk with her finger.

"Votan! You'll have to come in here to get it." Mary tore a paper towel from the rack in preparation for the dog.

Votan stopped to scratch as he came in the kitchen door. He didn't sit down but arched his long body and drew one scrawny hind leg under his chin.

"Eat that now. It isn't sour." Her voice was coaxing. Votan always held down his dish by planting a paw along its edge. Mary took the paper towel and tried to dislodge Votan's paw. He growled at her and pulled his gray lips back.

"Supper? Supper?" Robert called. At his words a great boom of thunder came. The lights in the house were whisked off. "Mary?" Robert sounded strained.

Mary got two candles from the shelf in the hall closet and took a lighted one to Robert's room. The trees outside were picking up the rush of the wind.

"Don't fix supper now." His voice sounded far away. It came evenly. Mary put the candle on his bed table and sat down in the softly cushioned chair facing his bed. Branches were snapping from the trees outside and cracking against the slats of the shutters. Robert had closed his eyes peacefully when he saw her sit down. Mary watched the rain flooding across the window by Robert's bed. The light of the candle reflected there made her glance back to watch his flame. Behind the candle a whirling pattern of light was playing on the wall. Mary watched the circles fuse and new circles form. Her head grew giddy and she could not draw her gaze from the motion. She might be very young now, she thought. "It is too dark to see," she whispered to herself.

The flickering design made her think of moving over the ground in autumn. One autumn years before, she had seen colored leaves sweeping by her feet and had felt the heat of a bonfire breaking through a crisp dash of wind. There had been a man, Robert, in a heavy grey sweater slashing down with his hatchet at a huge dark tree trunk. He was swinging his weight evenly and, at the same moment, passionately. His strength had encircled them. His clear blue gaze had met her when the logs lay quietly severed.

"Woman, I'm growling with hunger. Let's get to it!" He had watched her smile and flashed a roaring look with his silent eyes.

Mary remembered that the kitchen had not needed painting then. It had been shining yellow as he had wanted it to be for them.

She saw the peeling wallpaper where the circles of light had been moving. Her stare was broken by it. She turned her head to look at Robert, lying sunken into the mattress. She could not see his features.

The lights flashed on without her realizing it. She was searching for his eyes. He blinked in the light and said, "It's over now, isn't it?"

"Yes," she said quietly, still wanting to see the blue eyes that were now dim. She got up and pulled a blanket to his chest.

"Mary?" his voice pleaded.

"I'll get your supper now," she told him and staggered a little, trying to hurry from his room.

The next day it was much colder. The fence around the henhouse had been knocked down beneath a fallen tree. Mary gave up trying to dislodge the tree and improvised a fence with some wooden stakes and chicken wire. While she hammered the stakes into the soft earth, Mary kept looking toward the swamp. She wanted to walk to its edge to see the wild home of the fox. She pictured him running, never lying beneath a still bush, but a red flash coming beautifully to the gray swamp.

Robert had a temperature that morning and she had to keep watching him and give him his pills and cold water to drink. "Where ya been?" he asked her each time she came to his room. She felt guilty when he said it. She tried to explain to him about the repairs, and he watched her without nodding his head.

When she brought him his eleven o'clock pill, he balked. "Can't take it—bitter as gall." He turned on his side. "Don't be a child!" she begged him. As she leaned over him, Mary noticed the squawking of the hens. At first they only cackled to each other. Then they loosed shrill cries hysterically.

Robert looked at her knowingly. "Damn fox," he said.

Mary went to get her coat. "Votan!" she called. She saw the dog lying in front of the kitchen door, his hind legs spread out like a frog's. "Votan! It's the fox, boy—the fox!" She tried to incite him. "Come on—get him, get him, boy." She ran to hold the back door open for Votan. The dog stretched himself into a stand and eyed her with boredom.

"Go out, Votan!" She clapped her hands at him. "Quick! Quick! Chase him!" She pushed the long dog through the door with both hands and slammed it after him. In a moment she heard him whining and running his long nails over the screen.

"Votan. Where's my . . ." Robert called.

The chickens screeched more spasmodically now. "They'll all be slaughtered," Mary told herself angrily. She went to the hall closet and got Robert's shotgun.

Votan was thrown back as she came through the door. She walked toward the gate of the chicken coop, lifting the gun carefully. The red moving along the side of the hen house startled her. It turned and sniffed the air. She had never seen the fox so still before. She could smell the cold, stale death of Robert's room. Then she thought the fox was waiting for her. In a second she drew herself up, leveled the gun and shot. The fox reached forward with one quivering front paw as if to dash away, then dropped into the mud. Mary stood with a throbbing head. She wanted to give herself some sharp physical pain.

Mary turned back to the house feeling her coat heavy on her shoulders. "You are a damned responsible person." She spat out the words, gripping the gun hard into her palms. She threw her coat off onto the kitchen table and propped the gun beside it.

"Where's my Votan?" Robert called. Mary looked through the kitchen window hoping not to see the fox. There was Votan, scrutinizing the body of the fox from a distance. He stealthily approached and began to sniff around the fox's head.

"Votan!" Mary snarled the words and grasped the gun in her hands. She walked straight to where she had stood before, burning red inside with the red of the fox, blazing red inside with the red surging through her. She heard a shot and let the gun fall, horrified. Votan's blood was thick and red.

CHALMERS S. MURRAY, a free-lance writer now living on Edisto Island, is the author of two published books—a novel, *Here Come Joe Mungin;* a history, *This Our Land;* two stories published in *The Georgia Review* and another which recently appeared in *The South Carolina Review;* numerous newspapers features, and folk tales on the lore of the South Carolina lowcountry. He has lived in Georgetown, at which time he edited a weekly paper and corresponded for the *New York Times* and three press associations. Later in Charleston, he served as a reporter for the *Charleston Evening Post* and the *News and Courier.* He is married to the former Faith Cornish, whose paintings have been shown throughout the United States.

God Use Both Hand

(Note: In the Gullah dialect only the singular form is used in expressing number, hence "hand" for "hands.")

It was almost closing time when Dingle Miller came blowing and puffing onto the store porch. I heard him mutter, "Thank God I make it. Narrow squeak, all right."

His large frame filled the doorway, blotting out the light of the dying sun. I saw a quarter piece glittering between his thumb and forefinger. He waved it at me, and said with a grin, "Hold on a minute, Mr. Murray. I got some shopping to do. The pot on the fire, the children crazy-hungry, and my wife rearing to cook."

I had planned on going home early for I was weary of doing nothing. Since opening up shop that morning I had only taken in a few cents over four dollars, which represented a profit of about forty cents. I was feeling so blue that all I wanted was my bed and a good book, and then a deep sleep in which to bury my worries. But now that Dingle was here things seemed a little brighter. With the spending of his money would come one of his tales, and the long dreary day might end with a small glow after all.

I hadn't seen Dingle in a week and sensed that he had stayed away because his pocket book was empty. I had given him all of the credit I could afford, and he was too proud to beg.

After he had stored his purchases in his burlap bag he turned to me and said with another grin, "You want to know how I come by that money?"

I said, yes, indeed. I was glad to hear how anyone could find money in these black days of the Depression.

Well, Dingle said, this is how it happened:

That morning his wife, Marion, came to him with tears in her eyes. She reminded him that he had "eight head" to feed, and there wasn't a Christ thing in the pantry but a quart of hominy grits. Only one copper was left in the coin bag in her bureau drawer. Starvation was walking through the land, and soon Death would knock on their door.

Dingle reproved her. "Don't talk like that," he said. "All God promise you in this world is a living and a killing. As long as you on earth He will open the path."

He told her he had talked with God a little while back. God had come right out and said, "Take up your net and your line and go down to Townsend Landing. You will find a boat there. Row out into the deep and drop your line. You will come home with plenty of fish."

Dingle said he talked back to God soft-like. "God you know I ain't got no boat, and anyhow the water all stir up. Scarcely a dog fish bite now."

But God said, "Never mind. Do as I command."

So Dingle took up his net and his line and went down to the landing. There he saw a boat cocked up in the mud. He didn't ask himself how it came to be there, or who owned it, and why the oars were at hand. He just shoved off and rowed in the direction of "Tabby drop."

Tabby, as all Edisto fishermen know, is a celebrated drop off the ruins of a chimney built of oyster shells and lime in ancient days. If any fish bite, why they bite by "Tabby."

As he rowed along, Dingle said he tried to think if he had done anything that might bring him bad luck. He made a quick check. He hadn't turned back, nor talked with an old woman before setting out, and certainly there was no food in the boat to make the fish believe he wasn't hungry.

When he reached "Halfway Gutter" he rowed up alongside the bank, took the oars into the boat, and let the tide carry him. Then he got his net ready. In the first cast he drew in three shrimp. His heart sank. He cast again, and this time nothing came from the deep. Maybe God wasn't with him after all. But the third time he pulled in a cupful. Soon he had all of the bait he needed.

Again taking up his oars he started out for "Tabby." The sun was beaming hot, but the breeze was fresh. Dingle took off his old felt hat with the scolloped rim, and let the breeze blow on his face. With the coolness came a deep feeling of peace and contentment.

All signs were right. The water shined and glistened like cut glass. White foam ran along the shore. The wind blew soft and sweet from the south.

Dingle wheeled his line over his head, once, twice, thrice, and turned it loose. It struck the water two feet from the shore and settled down on an oyster shell bottom. A little swirl ruffled the surface and Dingle knew a bass was feeding nearby. He sat still and waited. Soon he felt something nibble like a crab. He pulled back his line about a foot and waited again. A bass struck his line so hard that the line almost cut his fingers.

"No use to fight, Mr. Bass," he called out. "God going to put you in my hand today, today."

The bass kept running. Now the line was nearly paid out, but just then the fish came quiet for a second, and Dingle began to haul in. He hauled strong but easy so the hook wouldn't tear from the bass' mouth. It was a big one with three spots on its belly. Down it plopped into the bottom of the boat and the hook fell out of its mouth. Dingle had been so scared that the bass would get away that sweat popped out on his forehead. He remembered saying then, "Thank you, Jesus, thank you very much. Creek is a blessed thing for we poor people. Looks like God put 'em there to feed the hungry."

Dingle stayed on that drop for almost an hour. The next fish was a catfish. He stored it in the stern for Marion. She was very fond of catfish stew.

Then a skipjack came over the side. He marked that for his sister's child, Maulin. The boy was so crazy about skipjack that he ate it down to the very eyes. Next came two croakers. Dingle marked those for

Susie and Pearline, his oldest daughters. He hadn't marked the bass yet. That was God's gift and he took it as a sign from heaven.

He moved from that drop and went down to John Jenkin's bank where the oysters bristled like hair on a hog's back. The first fish to come his way was a big whiting. This he marked for his two little boys. For once their stomachs would be full. Then the croakers started biting fast. He marked two for Daisy and Jewel and one for himself. Now the whole family was squared off.

After that six more croakers took the hook. They would furnish supper. Dinner was already provided. Dingle even caught a stingray. He marked it for Uncle Mike, who liked stingrays a lot.

After the stingray the fishing started slowing down, but he did catch two fair-sized whiting, and stored them away in the bow.

"Them been for my outside woman," Dingle explained. "I ain't tell God anything about that. God ain't want to know *all* your business."

About then Dingle saw a cloud rise from behind the salt marshes, inky-black on top and white beneath. In a little while the wind shifted and got into the cloud, and the squall broke. The boat rocked and pitched. Dingle rowed for shore as fast as he could and landed by the tabby chimney where he waited for the storm to blow over.

The thunder crashed and the lightning played all around him, and he prayed to God to save him from destruction. "God answer my prayer," Dingle said. "He put out He hand and shove the lightning off."

When the storm had gone a strange white man crossed the sand dunes and came down to the landing. He asked Dingle about his luck and Dingle showed him the big bass. The white man offered him forty-five cents for the fish, and Dingle took it. He never charged home folks but thirty cents for that size, but the man was an off-islander.

As Dingle shoved off in the boat ready to go home, he spread out the coins on the stern seat and made a division: Five cents for coffee, ten cents for lard to fry the fish in, two cents for kerosene to burn in the lamp, and three cents for horse cakes. "Children kind got to have something sweet to taste their mouth," he said.

Fifteen cents he set aside for a drink of whiskey. After that wetting he simply must have a drink to ward off chill and fever. Already the blue cold was seeping into his bones.

There was still ten cents left. Dingle said he had scratched his head and thought a bit. It came to him all of a sudden. The ten cents was for the collection plate on Sunday. That was God's share.

Business picked up a little following Dingle's visit. Maybe that happened, I thought, because his tale had put me in a cherful mood, and I could make myself more agreeable to my customers. But three days after hearing the story of Dingle's good luck, the bright picture he had shown me vanished.

The heavy footsteps pounded out a slow beat on the sagging pine boards, and I thought, That is old Ancrum Finney. No one else walks like that on the whole island. He's got something extra special to tell me, judging by the way he's stomping one foot.

All morning I had been thinking about a careless store clerk on the other side of the island who had sold poison to a customer by mistake, and had caused the death of three children. The instant I saw old Ancrum enter my store I knew somehow that his mind was on the tragedy.

"Good morning, Uncle Ancrum," I said. And then before he could return the greeting I burst out, "Wasn't that terrible about those three children. I suppose you've heard all about it by now."

Ancrum's voice answered, "Yes, I hear the way the people proclaim the story, but I know more than that. I been there myself the morning after the children fall sick, and I hear all the mummering talk of the people. They can't bring the thing out straight though, even with all the word they speak.

"Mr. DeWitt buy some rat poison three year ago. The rat been awful in the store then. You know how rat 'most carry *you* off 'less you fix some plan to kill the varmint.

"I been living over Big House side then, and I see the bottle myself. It look just like the bottle calomel come in—well almost. In the year the poison buy Mr. DeWitt have a clerk name Mr. Williams to help him. Mr. Williams he take the poison and lay it all around the jam of the store, then he take the rest of the poison and move it upstairs in the loft so nobody going to handle the bottle by mistake. Mr. Williams leave Edisto not long after that, and the poison just lie in the loft all that time. It pass clean out of remembrance.

"Ain't nobody for say how that poison get down on the shelf behind the counter. Maybe somebody pick up the bottle carelesslike and take it down stairs; maybe rat worry it around up there, and the bottle fall through a crack in the loft. Mr. DeWitt say he sure ain't pick it up. He say this to the judge, and the judge believe him.

"However it come about the poison been at hand that Tuesday evening. The way God fix it Moses Gathers come to the store that very evening to buy calomel for he children. Them children have pain in their belly 'most a week from eating too much meat gravy, and Moses say he got to buy medicine to drench 'em out. He make track for the store, and when he get there he ask Mr. DeWitt for calomel. It been just about dusk dark and the lamp ain't light yet. Mr. DeWitt say he been fumbling 'round, searching for match when Moses hurry in and call for the physic. Mr. DeWitt reach behind him where the calomel stay, and pick up a bottle and hand it over to Moses. Mr. DeWitt ain't look at the bottle, and Moses ain't stop to examine it either. Moses ain't know how to read anyhow, and he got something else on he mind.

"By the time Moses get home it been black night, and he wife mad with worriation. The children been crying and messing 'round like they crazy, and he take out the pill quick. He think the medicine go pacify them, so he take the pill and count 'em off—two for every child.

"The children raise rucas 'bout the medicine. They say the pain ain't so bad after all. Then Moses' old mudder step in. She take the bottle and study it close, then she proclaim something wrong. The bottle, she say, got elephant head on 'em like all bottle what hold poison. The old woman can't read no more than Moses, but she see the elephant head and point it out. Moses pay no 'tention. He say the bottle bound to be calomel 'cause Mr. DeWitt sell it for calomel. So he throw down one child after the other and choke the pill down.

"By and by the child name Ruth say she feel awful sick, and go off by herself. Next minute the boy, Caesar, fall on the floor and roll over and over. The third child also fall, but the biggest child hark and spit till one of the pill jump out his mouth.

"Moses scarcely pay them no mind till he see that Ruth got the fits, then please God he raise the alarm, and the whole house join in the shout. Time roll on and the children get worse. All take with the fits excusing the oldest one. That get next to Moses and he fly over to Big House to get Miss Sallie.

"When Miss Sallie come all three of the children stiff as board. The oldest one still breathe so Miss Sallie call for a purge. He take the purge and Miss Sallie roll him up in a blanket and put him in the Ford car. Then she sell out for the city. She give the others up for dead.

"Just as Miss Sallie drive off, here come Mr. DeWitt and Mr. King who live near Big House. Then all the colored people 'round about get there in a bunch, and the house full up with their noise. Mr. DeWitt take a good look at the children and say the breath of life ain't blow out yet. He holler to Mr. King to ride quick as he can for the doctor, and Mr. King do so.

"But please God when Mr. King get to doctor house the doctor ain't home! He been 'cross the river hunting.

"When the doctor do come he pronounce children dead. Soon as he say the word a big shout go up. The woman throw she apron over she head, and scream. 'Oh, Lord my chillun gone, my chillun gone!' Four other woman cry out, 'Yes, the chillun gone. The death angel afflict this house today!'

"Then Moses stand there by the three dead children and start to growl. He say Mr. DeWitt got to pay for the death 'cause he sell the wrong medicine. And there was mummering and muttering in that house that day. The woman cry till I think my heart going to crack in two. And Moses ain't change he tune. He stay on that one thing; Mr. DeWitt got to pay 'cause he sell the poison that bring the children down.

"Some of the people in the house speak the same word as Moses, but someday he better shut his mouth and take what God send on him.

"Yes, I been there myself, and I hear all the mummering and muttering, but I hold my tongue. Moses he keep right on talking from the house to the grave, and right from there to the courthouse. But Mr. DeWitt talk to the judge too, and the judge believe him.

"Maybe Moses still talking. I ain't been over that side since so I don't know for certain. All I know is the children been in the grave now three day with the earth jam down on their face."

LYNN ROSMER is a Charlestonian and graduate of the College of Charleston, where she was a frequent contributor to its literary magazine, *The Phoenix* (in which "The Furnished Room" first appeared). Her short story, "In the Forest of the Night," won the literary magazine prize for fiction in 1964. Her interest in writing began when she was seven, and she has been writing ever since. She attended the University of South Carolina College of General Studies' Creative Writing Workshop, where she studied under Richard Coleman. A story taken from parts of her current novel, "Stranger Here," was recently accepted for publication in the *Anthology of Negro Youth*.

The Furnished Room

"Mr. Pennington," the voice called. "Mr. Pennington, I know you're in there. It ain't no use trying to fool me. I can hear you breathing."

James stopped breathing and waited, holding his breath. Every time before she had gone away. He prayed for her to go away again.

"You can't fool me," she said. "I know you're in there. You want me to have to take legal measures? I got recourses, you know. I got recourse to the law."

Her voice assaulted his sleep like the voice of the Furies. He tried to steady his mind, to make it a rock that the voice would flow around, not disturbing; but then there was a new sound, a loud scratching, and with a vague, detached interest he saw a piece of celluloid come through the crack in his door and make the latch lift as if by itself. The door swung open and his landlady stood silhouetted, her head haloed in the light from the hall.

The room was too dark for her to see into at first, even though there was a workable light bulb hanging by a cord from the ceiling. The only light came from one window opposite the door, passing through a panel of stained glass leaned against it and slanting in dim reds and blues across the uneven, paint-peeling floor.

"Mr. Pennington?" the voice said. It was a different tone now, the hushed, questioning tone of an awed child. It was several moments before her eyes adjusted to the light and she saw James. He was in bed in his overcoat and gloves, propped up on pillows and with the blanket drawn up to his waist.

"Oh, I didn't know you was sick," she said. "I just come for the rent money, that's all. You know, it's gotten to where you can't trust nobody nowadays. You got to keep after everybody."

Half of his face was in shadow. A patch of blue light fell on the other half and gave the two parts a disconnected look like that of a shattered window in a ruined cathedral. She leaned forward and peered at him more closely. There was several days' growth of beard on his cheeks, and at the corner of his mouth she could see a faint tracing of white like a child's milk moustache half wiped away.

One glance around the room told her all she needed to know, and she began to smile.

"You know, I never figured you for a drinking man," she said, adding quickly, "not that I mind a man having a little once in a while if he's quiet like you and don't make no trouble. Some of my gentlemen has had me in for a drink occasionally, and I don't mind so long as they re-main gentlemen, like you. You know, I had you figured for a real gen-tleman right off, as soon as you come up to my door wanting a room. I thought to myself, 'He's either a preacher or a college professor; and if he ain't now, he has been.' I can always tell."

"How much?" James asked. His voice was dry and scratchy as if he hadn't spoken for a long time.

"Beg pardon?" she asked.

"The rent . . . How much." James said.

"Thirty-five, Mr. Pennington, and you might want to pay in advance for the next month. Some of the gentlemen like to pay in advance so they don't have to worry theirselves about it later. I wouldn't of both-ered you if I had of known you was under the weather, but you know how it is. You got to make ends meet. I been on my own since I was fourteen—owned a restaurant when I was eighteen—and I know it's a

bon sitting on his Oshkosh, and he went over and picked one up. He could see that he was holding it, but he could not seem to feel it; and while he watched, the bottle slipped from his hand and fell with a crash to the floor.

"Jesus H. Christ," Grace said. "Now look what you went and done."

"Yes," James said. "I couldn't . . . feel . . . anything in my . . . hand."

"Let me see," she said. She took his hand for a moment and said, "It slipped out on account of the gloves, but never mind, you just let little Gracie make the drinks."

"But I . . . couldn't . . . feel . . . anything," James repeated dully.

"You can feel my hand, can't you?"

"Yes . . ." James said. "It's like it was the last time. It comes and goes," he thought. Her hand was unpleasantly hot, even through the gloves, and he drew his away and held it close to his chest.

"Well, you just let me tend to the drinks. I'll have this out of the way before you know it." She swept the pieces of glass aside with her foot.

"Thank . . . you. I . . . appreciate it very . . . much."

He backed away from the broken bottle and noticed that the door was partly open. He moved to close it, but she laughed and said, "Oh, don't worry about that. They ain't nobody here besides us but Debbie, and she can't see nothing."

Debbie was the landlady's five-year-old blind daughter, a pale, whiny child who made him feel vaguely uneasy whenever he saw her, although he was ordinarily at ease with children. Once, while standing in the shadows under the stairs waiting until he could slip past Grace's open door and up to his room without having to speak to her, he had overheard her telling a friend, "She was born in the ladies' lounge of the Greyhound Bus Station in Newport News, bless her heart. I didn't have no silver stuff to put in her eyes. I didn't know you had to put stuff in their eyes. Her eyes looked all right—so pretty and blue. I guess I should of had her at the hospital, but I never did like all those nosy personal questions they ask you like you was trash."

James often heard the child walking up and down the narrow corridors, feeling her way by patting the walls. Once he had been standing in his doorway as she came by, and in passing she had put her hand on his thigh. He did not like to be touched, and he drew back so suddenly that she lost her balance and fell down. Immediately, she began to whimper; and, ashamed, he had gathered her up in his arms, making himself hold her as close to him as he could, put his lips to the knobby skinned knee, and said the formula he had always used for minor injuries on his younger brother, "I'll kiss it and make it well." When he set her on her feet again, she was smiling at him for the first time, and she had gone bumping off down the hall chanting tunelessly, "Kiss it, make it well."

"I don't know how you like yours. . . ." Grace was saying.

"Straight . . . please. . . ." James told her.

"I could tell right off you was a straight drinker," she said, handing him a glass half filled with whiskey. "I am myself. I've never seen the use of paying out a lot of money for good bourbon and then watering it all down. Jimmy—the other Jimmy—used to say if God had of meant good liquor to be all watered down, He would of made it that way. Jimmy had a real way with words. He wasn't serious and slow talking and quiet like you. It was always a gas with him. Of course, he didn't have such a intelligent vocabulary. I declare I wonder sometimes where you pick up so many long words."

"My mother was frightened by a dictionary before I was born," James said without smiling.

"Well, I swear!" Grace said, laughing so that her whole body shook and he had to look away. "I swear! You're a gas, too, in your own way, aren't you!" She took a long swallow from her glass without seeming to pause either in her laughing or in her talking. "You know," she said, "I hope you won't take this the wrong way, but you know, you're a very . . . attractive man. What I mean, distinguished looking like a preacher or a college professor. I mean, if you kept yourself up. You ought to keep yourself up better. You could get yourself a pretty young bride. You know, being so attractive looking and being a real gentleman"

James' face was so hot he felt as if he would faint if he could not sit down, but there was no way to sit without inviting her.

"Won't you . . ." he said lamely. "I haven't . . . much . . . furniture. . . ."

He started to move the books and empty bottles from the only chair in the room, but she had already settled her hips on the foot of the bed and crossed one thick thigh over the other. James, holding his glass carefully in one hand, moved a pillow between them and sat down stiffly.

"I hope you don't mind my getting a little personal," she said. "I feel like I can tell you these things since I must be so much older than you."

Again James knew what was expected of him, and his voice came back to him dully. "That's hard . . . to believe."

"Oh, all you men are flatterers," she said, "but, you know, you'd be surprised how few men are real gentlemen. You know how I knew you was a real gentleman? Not just show?"

"No," James said. "I don't."

"Well, when you'd pass me in the hall—when we'd have to pass each other and the hall'd be so narrow—you'd turn your back and go by instead of trying to embarrass me like the other men. At first I'll admit I wondered how come you was different; and then when I got to know you better, I said to myself, 'He's just a gentleman with manners and not like those other goddamn bums that are always trying to get away with something.' "

James took a long drink from his glass.

"I didn't think it was because you didn't find me attractive," she said, putting her hand over his.

He gently freed his hand, stood up, walked to the bureau, and set his glass down. Then with his back to her he said, "I find you a . . . very . . . attractive . . . woman, but I have to tell you . . . I'm . . . not . . . well."

"You mean you got something wrong with you?" she asked.

"I . . . have a . . . sort of a . . . block," he said. "My father is a . . . minister. When I was . . . twelve years old, I . . . cleansed . . . myself of all . . . desire for . . . women. When I was thirteen . . ."

"You did what?"

"When I was . . . thirteen . . . I cleansed myself of all . . . impure thoughts. I was going to be a minister . . . too. Then my . . . dreams . . ."

"No kidding. How'd you do it?"

"I . . . beg . . . your . . . pardon?" he said, turning.

"How'd you do it, preacher?" Her voice was hostile, and he remembered, " 'Hell hath no fury . . .' "

He thought for a moment. "I . . . lay . . . in bed . . . flat . . . with only my . . . head raised . . . and read a book . . . Lives of the . . . Saints . . . and I would get so . . . tired. I never . . . dreamed. . . ."

She burst out laughing and said, "Oh, Jimmy, you're a gas! I should of known you was just pulling my leg. You know, that's the thing I like about you. You got this sense of humor."

James smiled uneasily.

"You hot?" she asked suddenly.

"I . . . beg your pardon?"

"Aren't you hot? I don't see how you can stand it in here with a heavy coat and gloves on."

"I'm not . . . dressed . . . very well," James said.

"Oh, don't you worry about that," she said, rising. "You just make yourself comfortable, and I'll get us another drink. What was you in the hospital for, if you don't mind my asking?"

"Penance," James said. "I was a . . . stigmata case."

"What in the world's that? Some kind of back trouble?" she asked. "Don't you want to take off your gloves?"

"It's . . . I had some . . . very . . . unattractive . . . injuries to my . . . hands and . . . feet. I don't take my . . . gloves . . . off . . . ever."

She looked at him with interest. "You mean you never take those gloves off? You sleep in them and everything?"

James nodded. "And . . . everything."

"You know," she said, taking his glass and pouring them each another drink, "that reminds me of a show they had on TV. The late show, I think it was. Four—maybe five years ago they showed it. Anyhow, there was this man—I don't recollect who played him. He wore white gloves all the time and played the piano; and it turned out this doctor had sewed somebody else's hands on his arms so he could keep on playing, but it turned out they was murderer's hands and he had to keep on murdering. I've never forgot that show. Jimmy—the other Jimmy—said it was the best show he ever seen. You ever seen it?"

"No, I . . . haven't," he said, slipping out of his coat. "I haven't had much . . . opportunity . . . for watching . . . television."

"Well, it was a good show. You should of seen it." She handed him his glass and said, "You could hold it better if you didn't have them gloves on."

"Thank you," James said.

He watched her half empty her glass in one swallow and move around the room, first touching his stained glass panel and saying, "You know, this place looks like a goddamn church," and then stopping with one hand on her hip in front of the only picture in the room, a reproduction of a Grünewald crucifixion. "The man who painted that couldn't of loved Jesus," she said. "My little five-year-old blind daughter could paint better than that, bless her heart. It's just pure-T ugly. I wouldn't have it in my house. I don't see how you can even sleep in the same room with it."

" 'De gustibus . . .' " James said too low for her to hear. Her words were coming at him as if he were underwater; and even though he blinked his eyes, he could not get her clearly into focus. He kept one hand under his drink so that he would not drop it and stood trying to still a sudden sense of panic. He could not feel the glass in his hand or the rim of it when he put it to his lips. "Father, I can't . . . feel . . . anything. Father, I'm afraid. I don't want to be locked up again." His lips moved silently, and he could not have said whether he was speaking to his own father or to God. He only knew that the feeling was one he had felt once before. It was the time he had gouged the pieces of stained glass into his hands and feet and saw, but could not feel, the blood flowing. He had walked around the room three times in an erratic red circle with the glass in his feet and felt nothing and knelt and said, "Thank you, Father."

It was the same now, the same feeling of a clear plastic film around him, cutting sensations out, and he tried to feel by biting his lower lip;

but he couldn't tell, and he didn't want to bite until it bled. He didn't want her to see his blood.

"Please . . . touch me," he said suddenly, holding out his hand. "I felt . . . I could feel you . . . touch me . . . before."

She turned and came over to him.

"Are you . . . touching me?" he asked. He saw that she was. She set down her drink and reached for the top button of his shirt.

"You sure were slow," she said.

"No, you don't . . . understand," he said. "I'm . . . not . . . well. I can't . . . feel anything."

"You can with me, Jimmy, honey," she said. "Don't you worry."

Her hands were pulling his shirt free of his belt. "Listen. . . ." he said. He put his hands on her shoulders, held his breath, and briefly touched his lips to her forehead. "I don't . . . want to . . . hurt you, but I . . . have . . . troubles. Sometimes I get . . . alcoholic and . . . schizophrenic and . . . fanatical and suicidal, and right now is one of those times; and I'm . . . on the . . . edge, and every . . . move I . . . make is . . . mental . . . brinksmanship. I need . . . peace. I'm . . . not . . . well. You don't want . . . me. I'm not in a . . . condition . . . to make . . . love to . . . anybody. I tried to . . . once. It was a . . . failure. I had . . . auditory hallucinations and I was . . . impotent."

"You had what?" she murmured. She had pulled the shirt down around his wrists, and he had to shake his hands to free them.

"I heard a . . . voice . . . telling me not to, and I . . . couldn't."

"You can with Gracie, Jimmy, honey. I got the biting kind."

"It said, 'Thy . . . loins . . . are filled with a . . . loathsome disease. The wages of . . . sin . . . is . . . death!' I couldn't . . . make it . . . stop."

"Don't you worry," she said. "You just leave it to little Gracie." She pulled at his T-shirt and then drew back in surprise as a dirty, bent envelope that had been between his shirt and his skin fell to the floor.

"What the hell was that?" she asked.

"It's a . . . letter from my . . . little brother in . . . seminary," James said. "I . . . have a little brother in . . . seminary . . . John

Christopher . . . John, bearer of . . . Christ. He writes me letters
. . . asking me . . . if I am . . . outside of . . . God. That's his ex
. . . pression for it . . . outside . . . of God. He doesn't ask me . . .
right out. He asks me . . . what I am . . . doing . . . and if I am
. . . happy, but what he's . . . really . . . asking . . . is am I . . .
outside . . . of God."

"You never opened it," she said, picking it up and handing it to him.

"I can tell by the way he . . . puts on the . . . stamp. That's his
. . . saliva on the . . . stamp. I keep it . . . near me. It gives me
something to be . . . sane . . . for, something to be . . . impotent
for. So you see . . . I really . . . can't. I'm sorry. I . . . can't." He
turned away and set John Christopher's letter carefully on the bureau.
He hardly felt the blow that caught him on the back on the neck
instead of on the face as she had intended. It surprised him.

"You bastard!" she hissed.

He turned and saw her face so red and distorted with fury he couldn't
look at her. He closed his eyes.

"You filthy goddamn bastard!" she said. "I thought you was different
from the others. A real gentleman. Ha! I should of known. You're no
gentleman. You're nothing but a lowdown bastard like all the others.
Only worse. You think you're better than the rest of them. You come
in here with your long words and your 'yes ma'ams' and expensive
suits and treat people like trash. You think you're too goddamn good
to touch a woman. You do it with gloves on. You say 'touch me' and
then you act like you was talking to the worst kind of trash you could
throw off any way you like. Well, I'll tell you one goddamn thing, Mr.
Pious Prunes and Prisms Pennington. I don't care two red cents for
the whole lot of you. I been on my own since I was fourteen—owned a
restaurant when I was eighteen—and I seen my share of bastards. Let
me tell you, they ain't one of them's as big as he thinks he is. I don't
care for none of them. The only thing I ever thanked anybody for was
God because He made us women with a built-in way of making a
living, and that's about what I care for men. They ain't one of them
any different from any other. I keep the lights on so I can look at the
goddamn cracks in the ceiling. Men all think they're so big, but they

all do the same goddamn thing in the dark and treat you the same way. Except you. And you know what I think's wrong with you? I think you're nothing but a . . . dirty . . . filthy . . . pervert!"

James put his hands to his eyes. "I'm . . . sorry," he whispered. "I'm . . . sorry. I didn't . . . want . . . to hurt you."

He heard a strange gurgling sound and a protesting creak from the bedsprings, and he opened his eyes and saw with alarm that she was crying. She had collapsed in a heap on the bed, her round shoulders and breasts heaving convulsively, and she drew in her breaths in sharp, gasping sobs.

"Don't . . . cry," he said lamely, sitting down beside her and putting out a hand to smooth the hair away from the back of her neck.

She didn't answer, and her sobs increased. There was a raised black mole on her neck, and he drew in his breath and forced himself to lean over and kiss her there.

"You don't . . . understand," he said. "I don't . . . think I'm . . . better than . . . anyone. I . . . know . . . I'm not. I have to be . . . very . . . careful . . . to be . . . constantly . . . on guard. I have to . . . live with . . . myself . . . with God. It's very . . . difficult . . . for me. I am . . . constantly . . . in danger. When I was . . . in the . . . hospital . . . I couldn't . . . stand to . . . live with myself . . . much less with . . . Him . . . and they kept me . . . strapped down . . . to a . . . bed so I couldn't . . . harm myself. I came here . . . to be . . . out of . . . danger . . . to work with . . . glass . . . to not have to . . . communicate with . . . anyone . . . or . . . feel anything or be . . . anything but . . . unconscious. What I'm . . . trying . . . to say is I'm a . . . nut. I'm . . . off my . . . rocker. All my . . . screws . . . are loose. I'm . . . trying to . . . hold . . . onto myself, and it's an . . . effort at best . . . and it's an . . . a . . . frightening . . . effort, and right now I don't . . . think I'm . . . succeeding."

"I been on my own since I was . . . fourteen," she said between sobs, "and I ain't seen a . . . one of you that wasn't a bastard. Jimmy run off and left me when he found out I was in a . . . family way with Debbie. I rode the Greyhound bus all the way to Newport News in my condition in the middle of the hottest summer you ever seen

. . . and I made him beg me to marry him and then I said, 'Jimmy, honey, I wouldn't be your wife if you was the last living soul on earth, you bastard!' I don't give a damn for any of you bastards. All of you are . . . bastards. Except you, and you're a . . . crazy bastard. You think you can treat anybody like . . . trash. You got those Jesus scars on your hands and you think you're . . . Jesus."

"No, I do not . . . think I'm . . . Jesus!" James said intensely, almost hysterically. "I do . . . not . . . think . . . I'm . . . Jesus!" He could not tell whether he was talking to her or to the doctors at the hospital. "Please . . . listen to me . . . a moment," he said. "Listen to me and . . . tell me . . . if you think I . . . think I'm . . . Jesus. At the . . . hospital . . . they wouldn't . . . believe me. No one . . . believed me. They wouldn't . . . listen to me. They said I had . . . delusions of . . . grandeur and . . . thought I was . . . Jesus. Let me . . . tell you. Please . . . listen. Let me . . . My last year of . . . prep school . . . please listen. A boy accused me of being . . . homosexual. It wasn't . . . true. I have never . . . desired . . . anyone . . . that way. When I was . . . twelve . . . I . . . cleansed myself. It wasn't . . . true. But if I had denied it . . . they would have . . . expelled him . . . for telling . . . such a . . . lie. It was . . . him . . . or me. I let it be . . . me, and . . . they expelled . . . me . . . and . . . he never . . . forgave . . . himself. He . . . hanged . . . himself. You see . . . it was . . . my fault. It was . . . pride. Out of . . . pride . . . I let that poor . . . confused . . . lost . . . little boy take on a sin that he never . . . forgave himself for. . . . That he . . . hanged . . . himself for later. I . . . killed him and . . . sinned . . . very grievously. And I did it . . . just . . . so I could say, 'Look at . . . me. I am a . . . great martyr. They crucify me . . . and I forgive them and never say a mumbling . . . word.' I disgusted . . . myself. I disgusted . . . God. I was an . . . abomination. When they . . . told me what the boy had . . . done . . . when I realized it was my . . . pride . . . that had . . . killed . . . that boy, I . . . punished . . . myself out of . . . shame. That . . . was the . . . real reason. I . . . did it to . . . subject myself, to . . . make myself . . . suffer. Don't you . . . believe . . . me? I didn't . . . think I was . . . Jesus. God punished me with . . . madness.

'Whom the gods would destroy . . .' They kept me . . . sedated . . . in the hospital. I was . . . strapped down like an . . . animal. I don't . . . think . . . I'm Jesus. Do you . . . understand? Don't you . . . believe me?"

He was looking past her, his eyes moving frantically around the room like a trapped animal, and he did not see the quick flicker of triumph that came into her eyes.

"You think you're too good to touch a woman," she taunted. "You think you're Jesus."

For a moment he remained still, drawing in his breath unevenly, then slowly he reached for her and began unbuttoning her dress. There was no feeling in his hands. He undid her buttons the way he had undressed John Christopher as a child, fumbling a little now because he could not feel anything.

"Why don't you take your gloves off," she said, "if you don't think you're Jesus? You can't love a woman with gloves on."

"You mustn't . . . see," he said. "It's . . . ugly." He held his breath, reached up and pulled the light cord, and slowly peeled the gloves away from his hands.

"Are they off?" she asked.

James let out his breath. "Yes."

"Let me feel."

He held out his hands, and she took them in hers and moved her fingers over the scars.

"Oooh," she said and giggled.

When it was over, James lay rigid until the indecent creaking of the bedsprings had subsided in his ears. Then carefully he extricated himself from her, got up, and pulled on his clothes while she still lay stretched out on the bed with her legs entangled in the twisted sheets.

"What're you in such a hurry for?" she asked. "They ain't nobody home except Debbie and you and me, and Debbie can't see nothing, bless her heart."

James didn't answer. He located John Christopher's letter and slipped it into his shirt and then, on all fours, began patting the floor futilely for his gloves.

"You going to take a shower now?" she asked.

After a moment he realized she was speaking to him and answered, "Yes," without really having heard her question.

"To wash it off, huh. Don't you like me? Didn't you enjoy it?"

"Yes . . . I . . . enjoyed . . . it."

He needed air. He stood up and walked over to the window, pushed it up, and opened the shutters. Three stories down the street lights had come on, and a red neon sign in front of the house flashed

FURNISHED
ROOMS

in the dusk, staining the sidewalk beneath him at measured intervals. He closed his eyes so as not to have to see it and began breathing deeply. "Please, God," he prayed, "don't let me be sick before her." His hand was holding the wall for support, but he could not feel anything.

"You were good, Jimmy, honey," she was saying. "You waited for me real sweet. There's not many men will hold off for a woman like you done."

"I . . . held off . . . as long as I . . . could," he said.

He had held himself back, contained himself, waiting for a sign from her to tell him he had succeeded without committing himself and could withdraw; but at the last moment she had brushed her lips across his and said, "Oh, you sweet little Jesus man," and with a low moan of anguish and a long shudder of his body, he was gone.

"Oh, God," he prayed silently, gripping the wall until his fingers were white. "Oh, God, I'm going to be sick. I can't feel anything."

He felt the panic rising again. "Let me . . . touch you," he said, turning.

She held out her arms; and he went over to her, walking through the chips of stained glass without feeling them.

"You have . . . something on," he said, running his hands over her body.

"Not a stitch, Jimmy, honey," she giggled.

"I can't . . . feel anything."

Frantically, he began putting his hands to everything; the bed, the floor, the bottles, the suitcase, the glasses. Finally in desperation he pulled out John Christopher's letter and held it to his lips.

"I can't . . . feel . . . anything," he said again. "God has . . . struck me." He did not notice as the letter slipped from his hand.

"Whosoever shall offend against one commandment, he is guilty of all," a voice said clearly in his ear. "The wages of sin is death."

He turned on Grace. "Did you . . . say something?"

"I didn't say nothing," she said. "You hearing voices again?"

"No," James said. He told the voice silently, "I have sinned grievously against Him. Only He . . . can . . . absolve me, and I . . . disgust . . . Him." Numbly he walked to the window again, mentally composing a note to his younger brother. "Dear John Christopher," it said, then underneath, "Dear little brother in seminary John bearer of Christ I have kept your letter near me near my heart and now because I have offended against His holy law God has struck me and I can't feel anything again and I cannot live outside of God. Please forgive me if you can. Love, James." Once he had thought it, it seemed already written somehow and even received by his brother, and there seemed no need to write it down.

"There won't be any pain. I can't feel anything," he thought. He wished Grace didn't have to see him die, but he did not know what to say to her to make her go away without hurting her.

As he gripped the sill and started to raise his left leg, he suddenly heard a familiar bumping sound coming down the hall. "Mama," a child's voice whined outside the open door.

"Don't . . . let her . . . come in . . . here," James said. "I don't want her . . . in here . . . I . . . ."

"Oh, it's okay," Grace said. "She don't see nothing nor know nothing, poor little thing. I'm in here, Debbie, honey," she called to the child.

The small figure bumped in through the door.

"She mustn't . . . come in . . . here," James said, his voice rising.

He let go of the window sill and turned around. "You wait outside," he told her. "Your mother will be . . . out . . . in a . . . moment. You wait."

The child immediately sagged to the floor. Her lower lip slid out, and she began to whimper.

"You got no need to be short with her," Grace said huffily. "She ain't but a baby, bless her heart."

"You hush, Debbie, honey," she crooned, pulling the sheet up around her and reaching for the child. "You come here and recite for Jimmy what they learned you in Vacation Bible School. Show Jimmy how smart you are." She turned back to James and said, "She's blind, but she's smart as a whip."

"Please . . ." James said. He looked toward the window and prayed silently, "Dear God, have mercy . . ."

The child stood up, clasped her hands, and began chanting in a high, nasal monotone, "My name is Debbie Reynolds Rayburn. I am five and a half years old. I live at 113 Twelfth Street. ABCDEFGHIJKLM NOPQRSTUVWXYZ. 12345678910." Then tunelessly and without pausing she sang,

> "Jesus loves me, this I know,
> For the Bible tells me so.
> Little ones to Him belong,
> They are weak, but He is strong.
> Yes, Jesus loves me,
> Yes, Jesus loves me,
> Yes, Jesus loves me,
> For the Bible tells me so."

Grace engulfed Debbie in a kiss. "You got every line perfect," she said, "didn't you, honey."

Mutely, James slid his leg over the window sill. For an instant the pulsating sign below illuminated half of his face with a blood-red light, leaving the other half in shadow and giving the two parts a disconnected look like that of a shattered window in a ruined cathedral.

COOPER A. SMITH, a native of Cherokee County, teaches English in the Spartanburg City Schools. He has published a short story in the *Famous Writers Magazine* and articles in the *Gaffney Ledger,* Spartanburg's *Teacher Topics,* and the *South Carolina Educational Journal.* As a result of his writing, he received a 1969–70 Ford Foundation Leadership Development Program Award. He is married and the father of two.

Raghorn

I knew something was wrong the minute Dad sat down at the table. Mama knew it too, I could tell, 'cause she was silent. She put grits, eggs and livermush on our plates without a word.

Dad mumbled the grace almost without opening his mouth. Then you couldn't hear nothing but forks, spoons and plates rattling.

I kept my eyes right down in my plate. I didn't look up—and I don't think Mama did or Dad either. I was wishing somebody would say something. It was always that way with Dad when something went wrong. And me and Mama knew not to talk until he did.

Finally Dad said, without looking up, "That cow had a calf last night—a month early."

Still, Mama and I said nothing. It was never wise to crowd Dad with questions, especially when something was wrong.

"The thing ain't fully developed," he continued. "It'll be dead 'fore sundown, if it ain't already."

Mama said, "Well, we ought to try to save it, if—"

"Save that weaselly looking thing!" interrupted Dad. "Bury it!" And you could tell that settled it.

Nothing more was said about the calf—or anything else. I was wondering why it came early, and would you bury a live calf, or kill it or what, and wasn't that a terrible thing to do. But I wouldn't dare ask Dad. I'd wait to get Mama by herself and ask her.

After breakfast, I went to sneak a look at the calf. I was unlatching the stable door when Dad yelled, "Boy." That's all he ever called me, boy. "Boy!"

"Sir?"

"Can't you hear?"

"Y–y–yes, sir."

"You better act like it then. Come here." Dad was standing on the back porch. "Take that calf down to the bottom of the hill and throw it in that hollow or bury it, one. And get back here in time to catch that bus, you hear?"

"Yes, sir," I said.

It was seven o'clock. I had an hour to get rid of the calf and catch the bus.

I got the shovel from the tool shed, went to the stable and unlatched the door. Old Bessie was hovering over the slimy bit of flesh lying in the straw. She breathed on it, hunched it gently with her nose and made soothing sounds to it—all the while keeping an eye on me.

It was about the size of a cat and as red and boneless looking as the afterbirth beside it.

Staying close to the door, I tried to ease the shovel under the calf. But Old Bessie charged and chased me away. I went around to the other side of the stable, pulled her chain through a crack and tied her up close to the wall. Then I went back to the stable door and scooped the calf up on the shovel while Old Bessie strained at her chain and bellowed at me.

I went down the hill facing the morning sun, but it didn't seem like May anymore. I didn't feel right about taking Bessie's calf away from her. It lay across the shovel looking like a broken doll, its head and hind legs dangling.

I thought I saw it move once, but I figured it was me shaking the shovel.

When I got to the edge of the hollow, I took one look at the calf, braced myself, shut my eyes tight and drew way back like Dad does when he pitches a fork of hay on the wagon. I must have tilted the shovel, anyway the calf fell on the ground behind me.

I started to scoop it up again. But this time it really moved.

I squatted down and cautiously touched it with one finger. It was warm. Its side quivered a little and there was a twitching in one of its legs. A tiny blade of grass in front of its nose moved back and forth. It was breathing. It was alive.

I wonder did Dad know.

"Throw him in the hollow," he'd said, "or bury him, one." And I knew he meant dead or alive.

So, I clenched my teeth and scooped it up. Wishing I were somewhere else I drew back a second time being careful not to tilt the shovel.

But I couldn't do it. I thought of how Mama wouldn't like it and I remembered how Old Bessie'd looked at me when I took her calf away.

"I'll have to kill it," I said to myself. I got a rock bigger than the calf to smash his head. But I couldn't do that either. Trembling, I laid the rock down and tried to think.

It was about seven-thirty and Dad would kill me if I missed the bus. He didn't care that much about school, but I *had* to obey.

Obey or not, I couldn't bury that calf or kill it.

So, I took it into the woods and made it a bed of leaves by a big tree and covered it with brush.

I was glad Dad had gone to plow on the other side of the house when I came back to catch the bus.

I washed my hands, changed clothes and said good-by to Mama. She didn't even ask me about the calf. She just looked at me sort-a sad and sympathetic like. I guess she figured I'd buried the calf and wanted to forget it. She knew I wasn't much for things like that. Dad knew it too, but he wanted me to learn how to be a man like him. He always said I was a weakling and a sissy and he couldn't stand nothing weak. I guess that's why he didn't like the calf.

On the school bus everybody was yelling and screaming and acting the fool. Jack Higgins kept pulling Norma Jean's pig tails. The big boys were tripping up the senior girls and Johnny Taylor was ducking behind a seat stealing a smoke.

But that didn't bother me. I was looking out the window and thinking—thinking about Mama and Dad and the calf, and wishing I was real tough like Dad wanted me to be.

"I shoulda killed the calf," I thought. "Then he'd know I'm no sissy. He'd have been proud of me then."

I thought about the calf all day. I wondered if it would live till I got back from school.

When I got off the bus, I didn't even go by the house to leave my books. I took a straight shot for the woods and the big tree, running as fast as I could. Throwing my books on the ground, I raked back the bushes like a dog pawing for a bone.

It was still alive. I almost cried for joy, but I didn't have time, because it was panting and needed something to drink. Its sides went in and out like a hound's after a hard chase.

I put some of the bushes back over it, picked up my books and rushed up the hill to the house. Mama and Dad were in the field on the other side of the house planting corn.

I put my books on the kitchen table and fumbled in the pantry until I found the baby bottle Aunt Ella left when she visited us two years ago with Baby Joe.

Bessie'd been hitched out not far from the barn, so I wasn't long getting a bottle of warm milk. She didn't seem at all mad with me about taking her calf this morning. She just cropped grass and fanned flies with her tail while I milked.

I dashed back down the hill. And my calf had his first meal. With much hunching, tail-wiggling in the leaves and vain efforts to get up, it emptied the bottle in ninety seconds flat and wanted more.

But it'd have to wait. I wouldn't have time to make another trip to Old Bessie and back. Mama and Dad had seen the bus go by for sure and they'd be looking for me to eat, change and get to the field.

And that's what I did. We planted corn till dusk with me trying to figure out how to get back to the calf without Mama and especially Dad knowing it.

So when Dad told me to milk the cow and give the milk to the hogs (we never drank milk from a "fresh cow"), it was like throwing the rabbit in the briar patch; and when he cranked up the old Ford and went to town it was like thinning the briars out a little.

Old Bessie gave a gallon and a half of milk. The hogs got about a quart. I went to the woods, got the bottle from under the leaves where I'd hid it and me and my calf had a good time. It drank bottle after bottle until its sides looked like a basketball. Then it snuggled up in the leaves like Baby Joe in Aunt Ella's lap and went to sleep.

I covered him gently, hid the milk bottle and went to the house swinging the empty bucket back and forth through the weeds.

I cut wood, carried it in, locked up the henhouse and was drawing water when Mama brought Old Bessie to the well to drink. "Where'd you go?" she asked.

"Ma'am?" I said, coming out of my daydreaming and stopping the bucket about halfway from the bottom of the well.

"I saw you go past the hog pen. Where were you going?"

"Oh—er," I said, "I was taking some milk to the calf. It wasn't dead, Mama, and I just couldn't kill it." And I told her how I wanted to save it and teach it to walk. She didn't say so but I could tell she was proud of me . . . if only Dad were.

"Mama?" I said after pouring the water in the trough for Old Bessie, "Dad won't like it . . . will he?"

"If I know your Daddy, he certainly won't."

Old Bessie finished drinking, and tossing her head around to take a big swipe at a horsefly on her side, she slung water across Mama's face. She wiped it away with her apron.

"Mama," I started to say a second time, but Old Bessie drowned me out, bellowing three times right together as loud and as long as she could. I guess she was thinking about her calf.

"Mama?" I said again.

"Yes?"

"You won't . . . y–y–you won't tell Dad, will you?"

She just sort-a smiled and started back to the barn with Old Bessie. But that was good enough for me.

"Now I'll have a chance to show Dad I'm no weakling," I thought. "When I walk that calf back up the hill he'll be proud of me. He'll be glad I didn't bury it."

Every morning and every afternoon for the next three weeks I milked Old Bessie and took most of the milk to the calf. By now his legs were not as crooked and wobbly as they'd been and he could stand without trembling. I began to worry about him walking away and maybe falling into the hollow. So I found a rope, made him a slack halter and tied him to a tree. He didn't seem to mind.

Soon he was frisky, strong and beautiful with a glossy brown coat and a white spot right between his eyes and could drink milk right out of the bucket and eat grass. He learned to look for me and rush toward me as far as his rope would let him.

I was as proud of him as a father is of his son . . . well, some fathers.

It was near the end of May and school was almost out before I told Bud, Tommie, Kent and Ricky about my calf. You should-a seen their eyes! They had bicycles, scooters and dogs, and Tommie had a rabbit, but I was the only one with a calf.

They got off the bus with me that day after school, and we went tearing across the field straight for the big tree. They stood around with their mouths hanging open looking at my calf and me. I let it nibble my fingers and hunch me in the seat of my pants. I got down on all four and pawed up dirt like I hoped he'd do some day.

Then I lied and told them how my Dad had given it to me because it was so fine and healthy. And right then I could-a got all their bicycles, scooters, dogs, baseball mitts, Captain Marvel comic books and even Tommie's rabbit for my calf. They'd really look up to me now because nothing they had would ever be a bull.

When they left I sat on the damp ground looking at my calf. I named him Raghorn because Mama said that was a good bull name. And I thought so too. She showed me the picture of a white bull named Raghorn in a book by Longfellow.

"Raghorn, Raghorn," I said several times. But he just looked at me the same as before and kept switching his tail. I started to change his name but I didn't.

Three days later I untied him from the tree and took him to the house. He galloped up the hill and headed for the barn like he'd been planning it for a long time. And I guess he had; he'd heard Old Bessie bellow many times. I ran behind holding the rope. This was his chance and I was glad because it was my chance too—to surprise Dad.

I'd waited a long time for this; dreamed about it night and day, how surprised and glad and proud Dad would be to see the calf he thought was dead. And I'd be standing there grinning.

When we got to the barn Raghorn made a dash for Old Bessie, jerking the rope from my hands. She licked him all over and I thought he'd punch a hole in her bag.

I watched them and tried to rest from my run up the hill and calm myself.

Soon I wasn't tired anymore, but my heart wouldn't stop pounding because I kept thinking about how it would be when Dad found out about the calf. I couldn't wait. Before he was through sucking Old Bessie, I started pulling him to the shop where Dad was.

He was sharpening the mowing machine blade when I walked up. He took one quick glance at me and kept right on working. He didn't see the calf. I knew better than to bother him while he was busy, so I waited. My heart beat so hard it shook my whole body.

Finally Dad said, still filing away at the blade and without looking up, "What-cha want, boy?"

And my mouth worked but nothing came out. I swallowed hard and tried again, "Dad, I—I brought the calf home."

"You brought *what* home?" he said looking up with a frown on his face.

"The calf," I said. "The one you thought was dead . . . that Old Bessie had a month ago."

He looked at me, then at the calf, trying to get it all clear in his head. "Where's it been?" he asked. And his jaws began to tighten up.

"Down there in—," I said, pointing.

"I thought I told you to bury that thing."

"Y–yes, sir, but—"

"You didn't do what I told ya—did you, boy? You went to a whole lot-a trouble to make me out a liar."

"But I thought—"

"You *thought!* I didn't tell you to think. I told you to get rid-a that calf." He paused for a second, then in a low voice through his teeth said, "I ought-a make you kill it and bury it yet, just to teach you a lesson."

Tears blurred my eyes, rolled down my face and dropped on the front of my shirt. I started to walk away pulling Raghorn behind me. I saw Mama standing on the back porch, silent, watching me and Dad. She always got that way when Dad got mad.

"Keep that thing out-a my sight. You hear, out-a my sight," Dad yelled after me.

I didn't say "yes, sir." I didn't look back. I took Raghorn to the barn yard, tied him to a fence post, crawled up in the barn loft and cried myself to sleep on a pile of hay.

On the thirtieth of May school was out. For the next three months I did my part on the farm and tended to Raghorn—all by myself.

Soon it was September and school again. The year went by fast and I became a braggart about my bull and the envy of every seventh grade boy.

During all this time I'd taken special care to keep Raghorn out of Dad's sight. I hitched him out in the field on the east side of the house where there were no crops planted and Dad seldom went. He was the finest bull I'd ever seen.

I didn't say anything more to Dad about him, and although I know he looked at him when I wasn't around, he said nothing to me. I didn't like it that way. I still hoped that some day he'd say I'd done a good job with Raghorn, but he never did.

Raghorn was sixteen months old when the county farm agent Mr. Swink first saw him. "That's a mighty fine bull you got there, Tim," he said. "How'd you like to enter him in the livestock show at the county fair next month? He'd be sure to take a top prize. What about it?"

"Yes, sir!"

"Well you talk it over with your Dad. And if it's all right with him, I'll send a truck out to take him to the fair. It starts—uh three weeks from today."

"He'll be ready, Mr. Swink."

"You might get yourself two hundred bucks and a chance to take him to the state fair."

The next morning at breakfast I said, "I'm going to put Raghorn in the livestock show at the county fair. Mr. Swink said he'd win a top prize."

"That's nice," Mama said. But Dad said nothing. He just kept right on eating.

"Just wait till Raghorn takes first prize. Then he'll be proud of me and the bull," I thought.

Two days before Mr. Swink was to send the truck out for Raghorn, another truck came to our house. It came while I was at school. Mama told me about it when I got home.

I had come home whistling. Mama was waiting for me in the kitchen.

"Hello, Mama," I said. She spoke in a low voice and made a special effort to keep her back to me while she fixed my plate from the pots on the stove.

When she put my plate on the table her eyes were red. I believe she was going to wait until I'd eaten, but she couldn't keep it in that long. "Your Dad sold Raghorn," she said in a calm clear voice. "I tried to stop him but he wouldn't listen."

I couldn't talk or eat or cry. I just sat there blank.

"Maybe he'll at least give you the money," she said. "Talk to him when he comes back. He's gone to town now."

But I didn't want to talk to Dad or anybody. I left Mama sitting at the table with my untouched plate and walked down the hill where Raghorn had been hitched. Sure enough there was his rope lying in the grass with one end still tied to the peg. I went to the big hollow and looked in, and then to the big tree where Raghorn had his first meal.

I sat down idly tossing pebbles in front of me, remembering, thinking and wondering until way after sundown. Then I went to the barn, climbed up in the loft and tried to sleep. Mama came looking for me and begged me to come to the house and sleep. But I refused. I told her I'd come back into the house after this one night. She left, and I guess she told Dad. Anyway he didn't bother me—then.

I didn't sleep well that night. I turned and twisted and got hay down the collar of my shirt and had all kinds of strange dreams.

One was about a big brown bull the size of a horse. He was being chopped up into little pieces by a great big giant of a man who was throwing the pieces into a deep washed-out hollow. And there was a thin lady standing in the bottom of the hollow trying to catch the pieces.

The next morning Dad came out to the barn and roused me up with a plow line, just, as it seemed, I'd finally fallen into a deep, hard sleep. I climbed down out of the loft, bleary-eyed, and stumbled toward the house, Dad walking about a half step behind lecturing me on getting too big for my britches. He hit me around my legs and thighs five or six times with the rope—hard, blistering blows—but I did not cry. Seemed like all my feelings were gone.

I was too late to catch the school bus. So I walked to school and went about that day in a kind of trance, keeping to myself as much as possible.

When the last bell rang and school was out, I couldn't bear getting on that bus with all the teasing and questioning. So I left my books under my desk and walked back home down the railroad track.

It was nearly sundown when I walked into the yard. All was quiet, the Ford was gone. I knew I was in for a good whipping. But somehow I didn't care.

I didn't care until I heard the old Ford coming up the dirt road and saw the cloud of dust rising behind it. Then I decided I'd had my last whipping.

I quickly crawled under the house—all the way back to the chimney and lay there quietly on my stomach with my right cheek on the back of my left hand.

The car pulled into the yard and stopped. I saw the bottom of the door open and Dad's shoe step out on the ground and start toward the porch. Then I saw Mama's feet and legs come around the other side of the car.

"Maybe he's here by now," Mama said. Dad mumbled something. "If he's here, Brad, please don't whip him this time."

Dad said nothing to Mama. Instead he yelled, "Boy! you in there?" as he opened the door and went into the house. "Wait till I get my hands on that boy. He won't try this trick again." I could hear them walking all over the house, going to every room. I could almost feel Mama wishing and hoping he wouldn't find me.

Another car pulled up beside Dad's Ford. There was a light tap on the horn. And I heard Mama say, directly above me, "Maybe that's somebody bringing him home."

I saw Mrs. Jones' feet head toward the porch. Mrs. Jones was my teacher. I'd know her shoes anywhere.

Mom and Dad came out on the porch. "Yes, Ma'am," Dad said, "what can I do for you?"

"Is this Mr. and Mrs. Cross?"

"Yes it is," Dad said.

"I'm Mrs. Jones, Tim's teacher. I was out this way visiting some of my students so I brought Tim's books by. I guess he forgot them today."

"Where'd you find them?" Mom said.

"Oh, they weren't lost," said Mrs. Jones as she handed the books to Mom. "They were right under his desk where he left them."

When Mrs. Jones gave my books to Mom a paper fell out of my notebook, and I saw Dad's big hand pick it up. For the next four or five minutes while Mom and Mrs. Jones talked, Dad didn't move out of his tracks or say another word.

I heard Mom tell Mrs. Jones that I didn't come home from school. "We went to Mr. Sam's, the bus driver's house, and he said Tim didn't get on the bus," Mom said.

"He probably walked home with some of his friends," said Mrs. Jones. "Don't be too alarmed and don't be too hard on him. He is really a good student. You know we all get careless sometimes. But maybe you do need to talk to him. I'm sort-a worried about the way he acted in school today—as if he was in a daze—like something was bothering him. But I'm sure it's nothing to worry about. He's a very sensitive and intelligent boy."

Dad still stood where he'd picked up the paper that fell from my notebook, even after Mrs. Jones had gone.

Then Mom and Dad were left standing in the yard. Mom said, "What's that?"

"A paper," Dad said. "Something that boy–uh–Tim wrote for his English class."

"Let's see . . . What I Want More Than Anything Else," Mom said, reading the title of the composition. Now everything was quiet as Mom read my composition silently, and I think Dad read it over for the third or fourth time. I wanted to crawl out from my hiding place under the house and tear it up. I had written it three weeks ago. It said:

"More than anything else, I want my Dad to be proud of me. I want him to call me 'Tim' instead of 'boy' and help me dig bait and take me fishing. I don't care if I never get a bicycle or a jacket with a zipper in it or things like that, if my Dad would just be proud of me.

"But he says I am a sissy. Someday I'll prove to him that I'm not. I have a big bull that I raised all by myself and Mr. Swink wants me to enter it in the county fair, and when he takes first prize—or second prize—my Dad will be proud of me. That's what I want more than anything else in the world."

Mom left to water and milk Old Bessie and Dad sat on the edge of the porch with his feet on the ground and with my paper in his hands. He sat there quietly until way late up in the night. And I lay under the house as still as death.

About ten-thirty Mom came out of the house onto the porch and said to Dad, "Brad, don't worry; he'll be back." And I made myself comfortable in the dust and went to sleep.

ROGER PINCKNEY, from Beaufort and Columbia, is a graduate of the University of South Carolina. He has won the W. T. C. Bates Award for fiction and has published in the University of South Carolina literary magazine, *The Crucible*. He is currently enrolled in the University of Iowa Writer's Workshop and is seeking his Master of Fine Arts degree from that university.

Things that Vanish

. . . Although she strews the leaves of pure
obliteration in our paths . . . She makes the willow
shiver in the sun.
                                              —*Wallace Stevens*

The truck ahead loomed up out of the darkness, its brakelights flaring red. His own truck braked sharply and the boy heard a voice sing out "Put a man here!" but he was off and running, gun in hand, even before it had stopped rolling. His feet stung with their impact on the hard clay road. He stumbled, almost fell, but by gradually decreasing his pace, he managed to stay up. He slowed to a walk, then stopped and watched the two sets of taillights wink out of sight around a curve in the road, leaving him in blackness.

He took a cigarette from his pocket and lit it, walked to the edge of the road, groped around until he found what felt like a pine stump and sat on it. For a while that cigarette, those that followed it and the dull green glow of his luminous watch were the only sources of light, then from around the curve came the headlights of the returning trucks.

They rattled past him and were gone, one tooting its horn in recognition.

Minutes passed. A barely perceptible stirring through the woods told him that it was near dawn. Gradually the stirring became a breeze and he began to distinguish between earth and trees, between trees and sky. The east began to turn pink and streak up and it was day.

The woods became alive. To his left a mockingbird shuttled its notes through the needles of a loblolly pine and a thrush rioted in a scrub oak. Through the pines before him came the drumming of a wood-pecker; somewhere behind him a yellowhammer piped its lutelike song. At his feet a procession of ants was busily gathering breakfast, carrying bits of something into a hole at the base of the stump on which he was sitting. An inchworm was pulling itself along at right angles to the ants. He put out his foot across the worm's path. It eased up to the edge of his boot, raised up on its rear portion, hesitated, waving itself back and forth, then came down on the edge of the sole. It inched its way quickly across the top of the boot and started up the pants leg. Before it got to the boy's knee, he picked up a twig, let it climb aboard and set it down on the ground. Then he heard the dogs.

Their houndish bugling faintly drifted along the breeze, through, between and among the pines across the road. He could hear the short "chop chop" of the beagles and other smaller dogs mixed with the louder and lower baying and howling of the big walkers and black-and-tans. Their voices rose and fell alternatively and seemed to be tumbling over each other through the woods. He could tell by the excited pitch that they were running and he imagined Diana herself riding in front of them. The yelping grew louder for a minute or two then gradually died out as the dogs followed the deer upwind. Again he heard the lute song of the yellowhammer, the woodpecker's primitive cadence. The woods suddenly became greener as the early morning sun met its first cloud, but it was quickly back out again, making dappled patterns dance across his legs and lap and the gun that lay across it.

It was a fine gun, a German sixteen, given to him by his father as a graduation present. Engraved on one side of the receiver was a large shaggy-coated stag, with his head tilted back as if frozen in the midst of a mighty bellow; and on the other side was a smaller animal, probably a roebuck, caught by the artist in the middle of a kind of cantering jump. Underneath, on the trigger guard, was a fierce looking boar and the date 1914. Each animal was framed with clusters of oak leaves and ivy which covered the remainder of the gun's receiver. Ever since his father surprised him with it, it had occupied an honored place on his gunrack. Although he often carried it deerhunting, he had never drawn blood with it. He had used it on quail, of course, and on an occasional squirrel or two, but they can be quickly thrown into the gamebag and forgotten. Not so with deer.

He had his first brush with buck fever long ago. The dogs ran a six- or eight-pointer through a broom sedge field right to him, but he was so taken by the animal's grace and speed that he just stood there, gun in hand, with the safety on, while the buck run up to and past him, into the swamp beyond. The whole incident had taken on a dreamy quality in his mind. Afterwards, even he wasn't sure enough about it to tell it to any of the others on the hunt. Now it seemed that the buck was the biggest that he had ever seen; he remembered that it had snow-white antlers.

Somewhere out in the woods the dogs started up again. For several minutes the boy couldn't decide exactly what they were doing. They seemed to linger in the same spot for a while, then swing to the right, then back to the left again. Finally he decided that they were running directly toward him. Mingled in with the barking and yelping, he began to hear the whooping and screaming of the mounted drivers as they encouraged the dogs and frightened the deer. His hair began to prickle and his scalp tightened; his stomach knotted and his temples pounded in anticipation. He got up from the stump and walked across the road, into the edge of the woods beyond. Walking to the top of a little hillock, he scanned the woods in front of him. Several dozen yards away, a well-worn deer trail crossed a fire lane in the middle of a patch of low scrub palmettos. He figured the deer would run that trail so he planned to wait there.

He was almost there and looking down, picking his way through some briars, when he heard light, cantering hoofbeats on the path. Looking up, he saw one, long yearling doe coming toward him, running with her head down. He swung his gun on her and threw the safety off. She must have heard the small metallic "snick," for she raised her head and stopped, all at once. She stood there and looked at him, big-eared, tall and tense, lean and lithe, with brown eyes as soft as sleep. And he stood there and looked at her down the barrels of his gun, with that white ivory bead centered on those sleep-soft eyes. Time passed. He slipped the safety back on and slowly lowered the gun from his shoulder; the deer did not move. "He-yah," he yelled and stamped his foot. The doe took off like a released spring. She jumped to the side and crashed off to his left.

He was halfway back to the road when he heard the shot. He ran but he didn't know why. He knew well what one shot meant. Two shots could mean a miss, three almost surely did, but one left little room for doubt. He pounded down the road for a hundred yards, or so, and plunged into the underbrush. A branch lashed across an eye, blurring his vision long enough for him to take a tumble over a log, but he was up again in an instant. He arrived nearly exhausted and found what he had expected. His doe lay on her side in a leafy-floored clearing. On her front shoulder were half a dozen dark red spots where the buckshot had entered. Her head was tilted far back, exposing the flowing gash where her killer had cut her throat. Blood soaked into the leaves beneath her and already an obscenely bloated, blue black fly was buzzing and circling around. Her eyes were still open.

The hunter smiled at the boy and began wiping the bloody blade of his pocket knife on his pants leg. "Yessir," he said, "she'll make a mighty nice piece of meat. Does always do. Yessir, a doe or a yearling buck."

He walked slowly back to his stump and sat down, angry and confused. He sat there for a minute, then walked across the road to where he had first seen the doe. Two chase-worn hounds came whining and sniffing along the same trail as the doe, their feet whispering through the dry leaves. One stopped suddenly when he saw the boy and looked up questioningly the way a dog does when he expects a shot but doesn't hear one. The other ranged around in circles and figure eights trying to pick up the scent again. When he found it, he threw his head back and yelped joyously. The first dog joined him and both bounded off, barking and baying, in the direction the doe had fled. The boy looked down at the stag, preserved in steel in the side of his shotgun, absent-mindedly rubbing the engraving with his thumb. A stirring in the dead leaves at his feet made him glance up anxiously, but it was only a small whirlwind that came through the trees in front of him and passed on. A small chill started at the base of his spine and crawled up to the nape of his neck. He buttoned up the top of his hunting shirt and walked back to the road. The morning breeze had turned quite chilly; he looked up and was not surprised to find the sky an overcast gray. It would rain, he guessed, before noon.

FRANK DURHAM, a Columbian, is a professor of English at the University of South Carolina and has also taught at The Citadel, Clemson, the College of Charleston, and the University of North Carolina. He has been a Rockefeller fellow, a Fulbright lecturer in Australia, a Smith-Mundt lecturer in South Vietnam, and a fellow in the Cooperative Program in the Humanities. He is a former director of Columbia's Town Theatre and the Macon Little Theatre and has acted professionally on the stage and in television. The author of six published plays, Dr. Durham has also written essays, short stories, and poems which have been printed in this country and abroad. His books include *Dubose Heyward: The Man Who Wrote "Porgy," Government in Greater Cleveland,* the Sullivan's Island Edition of Poe's *The Gold Bug, Elmer Rice,* and *The Collected Short Stories of Julia Peterkin.* He is co-editor of *The South Carolina Review.*

Adamus Perplexus *

Monosyllabic wonder stirred his mind
At contemplation of the known concealed
Beneath the fuzzy leaf. So well defined
That spot in memory seemed; his senses reeled
Now in the fumbling, faded pictures which
Long intimacy breeds. How many times
She'd stood there in the sunlight, in the rich
Full glare of noon; but just the green of limes,
The dusky purples of the grapes she ate——
Prismatic blinders on his eager eyes;
And casual brush of moonlight he had late
Observed, now whispered tantalizing lies.
    She stood there by the violated tree,
    Stranger and wife and quintessential she.

* Buckler Sonnet Prize, 1954.

Infallibility *

The calf, O Moses, had a beauty, too.
Recessed somewhere within my human mind
It clings tenaciously. Truth lies with you:
You thundered righteously that we were blind.
Perhaps we were. 'Twas sin to bend the knee
In worship of that lovely gleaming beast
Which stood there auraed with divinity,
Its nostrils dilate, sensitive. The least
We could have done, God knows, was wait.
For you would come; you always have. You came,
Your eyes intense, with godhead agitate,
With graven laws that brought an icy shame.
     Have you forgot in Egypt once you fled
     And, human, left a man behind you dead?

* Book Basement Prize, 1952.

The Lamb *

The pure white lamb was born to know the thrust
Of sacrificial blade. Its flesh and blood,
So vibrant now with youth, at some day must
On altar stone or cruel cross of wood
And searing nails commingle with the prayer
Or curses of imperfect men who try
To please a god and save themselves. The heir
Of ancient cruelties must dearly buy
The patrimonial gift. Still, unperturbed,
The little creature frolics in the sun
Beside old Joseph's shop, but slightly curbed
By boyish hands or threats pronounced in fun.
    And in the shadow of an ancient tree
    The mother, watching, ponders silently.

* Honorable Mention, Poetry Society of South Carolina Competition; bought by *Letter* Magazine.

Her Father Loved Horses

I guess I saw Lula Mae naked more than a thousand times, but after the first time it didn't mean a thing to me. When she was about twelve and I was ten, we used to swim together in the millpond a mile from town and then stretch out under a tree to dry off and talk.

Lula Mae was lying there one day, chewing on a dandelion stem and telling me the reason why her mother was drunk so much.

"Ma always explains her drinking and says she's real sorry for it," Lula Mae said thoughtfully. "And when Ma's sorry she's so sad it near 'bout breaks my heart."

"But how does she explain it?" I asked.

"Ma always says she has a good reason for all that wild drinking she does," said Lula Mae. "And she sure has, I guess."

"But what reason?" I persisted.

"Ma's had two great tragedies in her life."

"What's a tragedy?"

Lula Mae looked at me patiently. "That's when you got great big trouble, so big that even crying won't drown it. Only whiskey, Ma says."

"What kind of big trouble has your Ma had?"

"Two tragedies," said Lula Mae. "Not just one. One's enough to weigh down most people more than they can bear. But Ma always says she's had two and is still standing up."

"Not when she's been drinking," I said.

"What do you mean?" asked Lula Mae.

"Not standing up," I said stubbornly. "Last Saturday night I saw her falling down in the ditch by Bransome's store."

"Oh," Lula Mae said, "that's just her body. But her soul is standing up straighter'n a pine tree. Ma says there's lots of folks walking around whose souls are flat down on the ground."

"But what are your Ma's tragedies?"

Lula Mae bit off the end of the dandelion stem with a little *click*. "Ma says Pa's dying was her last tragedy."

"And the other one?"

"It was her marrying Pa in the first place."

I'd heard Mother and Daddy talking about Lula Mae's family. They lived two doors from us, and before her Pa died we could hear all the fighting and yelling as clear as if it was in our own yard. Lula Mae's Pa, Mr. Sam Persons, was a disappointed man. He was a horseman. He'd come down from Kentucky with bunch of fine horses when the carriage was the most elegant way for a family to ride. For several years he ran a livery stable and did pretty well. Daddy remembered him dashing around town in a small-checked suit and a pearl gray hat and spats, sitting there behind a pair of matched bays and flashing a whip with a gold knob on it. It was then that Lula Mae's Ma (though she wasn't yet) had married him. She was Sookie Casford and poor as Job's turkey but pretty as a picture. For a while after the marriage they lived high, trips to the Derby and other big races, champagne, and steaks two inches thick. Mr. Persons laughed fit to kill when the first Stanley Steamer chugged down the streets of our town.

"It'll blow up, sure as hell! You just wait and see," he said.

Instead, Daddy told me, it was the horse business that blew up. But Sam Persons never believed it. He kept waiting around, his business dribbling away to nothing. The small-checked suit and the spats and the pearl gray hat got scruffy at the edges. Finally, Sam just sat at home in his bedroom and wouldn't talk to anybody. I remember seeing his pale face at the upstairs window, a face that stared out at the automobile-filled street. He must have been hearing the smart click of hoofs, the brisk snapping of a gold-knobbed whip, and the whir of shiny black carriage wheels.

Then one day Sam's face wasn't there any more. Mrs. Persons arranged for him to be carried to the graveyard in a horse-drawn hearse. But the horse was a sway-backed mare from the town garbage wagon. Sam wouldn't have approved of it.

At first people sympathized with Mrs. Persons and overlooked her drinking to drown her sorrow. But when she began hanging around Bransome's store and buying beer and corn whiskey and wine on credit, the ladies shook their heads.

"Poor Sookie," they said. "She sure must've loved Sam a lot in spite of all the fighting they did. But now it looks like she loves drinking even more. After all, there *is* a limit to mourning. Beyond a certain point, it can become—well—self-indulgence."

The men laughed. "Sookie's a souse," they said. "She takes the food out of that sweet little Lula Mae's mouth just so she can pour whiskey down her own throat."

And it was true. There was many a time when Lula Mae didn't really have enough to eat, and she wore the same little-girl dresses a long time after she was, to every eye, not a little girl any more. It made the men stare at her, busting out of her clothes as she was. But Lula Mae never complained. She always talked about it just as she did that day when we were lying under the tree beside the millpond.

Suddenly from the bushes behind us there came a great caterwauling, as if some creature was in awful pain.

"What's that?" said Lula Mae, rising up on one elbow.

"Sounds like something getting killed," I said, afraid.

Lula Mae was on her feet. "We've got to help it," she said and made a dash toward the sound.

I followed her, not very happy, as danger is something I prefer to avoid. And soon I caught up with her.

She was standing still looking at Moose McMany who was swinging a gray kitten by its tail.

Moose was about Lula Mae's age, but he was huge, a great big lunk of a boy with the brain of a mosquito and the muscles of a tiger. Most of the time he was real gentle and kind, and he liked to play with the little children. But sometimes, when he was teased or when the moon was full, some sort of evil spirit took over in Moose. He liked to hurt things.

Now he was swinging the kitten with a kind of silly grin on his face and drool running out of the corner of his mouth.

Knowing Lula Mae, I expected her to leap on him and fight him to rescue that kitten. She loved little animals and couldn't bear to see them suffer. But I didn't fully understand her.

She stood there looking at him with a real sad expression on her face.

"Hello, Moose," she said as gentle as you please.

Moose, his eyes sort of glazed, kept on swinging the kitten.

"Hello, Moose," Lula Mae said again, real soft, but firm.

Without breaking his swing, Moose turned his eyes toward Lula Mae.

"Hi, Lula Mae," he said, just as if he was meeting her on the street. But he kept on swinging the kitten, and the kitten kept on yowling, not so strong now as at first.

"What you doing, Moose?"

Moose looked surprised at her ignorance. "Swinging a kitten," he said slowly in that kind of bubbly voice of his.

"Why?" Lula Mae asked.

Moose thought a minute. "I don't know," he said, and his arm began to slow down a little in its circles. "I guess 'cause it's fun. Sort of."

"Not for the kitten," said Lula Mae.

Again Moose thought long and deep. He stopped swinging the kitten and held it in his big hand and looked at it. "Naw, I guess not," he said at last.

"Give it to me. Let me hold it," she said and reached out her hands.

Moose gave her the kitten, which was making a kind of dry whimper.

"It's so little and helpless," said Lula Mae, stroking its fur. "Just look at it, Moose. Ain't it sweet?"

Moose looked. Then he reached out a big hand, sort of uncertain, and began to pat the kitten, too. "Yeah," he said, smiling and looking as gentle as a calf. "Sweet."

In a minute the kitten was all right again and purring like a steam engine.

Lula Mae put it on the ground. "Now go home, baby!" she said and patted its little rear. It twisted around her leg meowing for a second; then it scuttled off through the bushes.

Moose and Lula Mae watched it go. Then Moose turned and looked at Lula Mae. His eyes filled with wonder.

"You're nekkid, Lula Mae? Ain't you?"

"Yes, Moose," she said.

"Why? Why, Lula Mae, why are you nekkid?" He looked puzzled.

"Bo and I been swimming," she said matter of factly.

"Oh," said Moose, satisfied.

"Lula Mae," I said, "don't you think we better be getting dressed? It's almost time for dinner."

"Yes," she said and started back toward the millpond. "Good-bye, Moose."

"Good-bye, Lula Mae," he said amiably. And he looked after her as she stepped into the bushes.

I followed her, and I found I was covered with sweat. I sure wouldn't like to tangle with Moose when he was in one of his bad spells.

Suddenly through the bushes behind us came Moose's bellow. "Lula Mae!"

"What is it, Moose?" she called back.

"Lula Mae," he hollered, "you sure are pretty."

"Thank you, Moose," she answered and stepped on toward the millpond, her feet hardly disturbing a leaf.

As we were dressing, I said, "Lula Mae, why ain't you afraid of Moose? He's twice as big and strong."

"I ain't afraid of a baby," she said. "And Moose is just a baby. He don't mean to be cruel. He just don't know any better."

"But he could've laid you out with one swing of his fist."

"He won't," she said. "Not if you're gentle with him. He's like most people and animals. If you try to bully them, they'll fight back at you. But if you're real gentle, they'll be gentle, too. Moose ain't really mean. People just don't understand him."

I hoped Lula Mae was right. Because if anybody did actually tangle with him, Moose could make mincemeat of them. And then, too, since his Pa, old Elk McMany, had come into all that Louisiana oil money, he thought he could buy anything. Elk once paid Jim Sanders for a chicken Moose set fire to, so much that Jim Sanders was wishing Moose would burn up a few more chickens.

Luckily, Moose was good-natured most of the time, and when he wasn't he generally picked on cats and dogs and occasionally a calf, not people. So his escapades didn't cost old Elk very much.

Not until the last one. But even then Elk got off lighter than he should have.

It happened when Lula Mae was just turning seventeen and was so pretty she took your breath away. Her Ma hadn't let her go to high school, so I didn't see Lula Mae as much now. Not even in the afternoons when I was free, because she was clerking in Bransome's store. Not that Lula Mae ever laid hands on any of the money she earned. Her Ma's grieving saw to that. Old man Bransome said he gave Lula Mae the job so that he could realize a little something from all the beer and corn whiskey and wine that Mrs. Persons was charging and never paying for. So Lula Mae worked at the store, and on Saturday old man Bransome took her mother's drinking for the week out of Lula Mae's wages. Most of the time Lula Mae owed him money.

When I asked her about it, she said, "I just have to help Ma. You don't understand, Bo, what it means to have *two* tragedies in your life. I just have to."

There wasn't any arguing with Lula Mae, even for her own good, when her heart had been touched. So I gave up and just dropped into the store to chat with her.

Moose did, too. Drop into the store, I mean. He wasn't much on chatting, but he used to hang around staring at Lula Mae and sort of grunting. Now he was as big as an elephant and not one-hundredth as smart. His bad spells came on oftener, and he seemed to be working up to something, hurting something bigger every time. Seeing him in the store drooling over Lula Mae used to make me sort of shiver.

I told Lula Mae so. "It ain't safe," I said. "Moose is all wrong in the head. I don't like the way he gapes at you. He's dangerous."

"You're crazy, Bo," Lula Mae said and laughed. "Moose is just a big baby, and I am no more afraid of him than anything. He always does exactly what I ask him, if I'm gentle with him."

"Some day he might not," I answered. But Lula Mae just smiled.

Then one day they found Sara Sanders, Jim's ten-year-old girl, with her neck broken.

Beside her they found a tennis shoe big enough for Noah's Ark, and on the inside was written in indelible ink "Erasmus McMany." I had forgotten that "Moose" was just a nickname.

And now Moose had disappeared.

Fortunately, Sara wasn't dead. But she wasn't very much alive either, at least not enough to talk.

"It's just plain accident that my boy's shoe was lying right there beside her," announced Elk McMany to the crowd at Bransome's store. "Just plain accident. It don't prove a thing. Moose is always leaving his stuff around, you know that."

"But where is Moose?" asked old man Bransome. "He ain't been in the store all day. And you know that ain't natural."

"Now let's everybody simmer down," said the sheriff, standing next to Elk. "That shoe is just purely circumstantial evidence. It ain't no proof that Moose was anywhere near when that sweet little girl fell and broke her neck."

"How do you know she fell?" asked old man Bransome.

"It's just logical," said the sheriff. "This is a peaceable neighborhood. We ain't got no stranglers lurking around."

"Sure, he ain't lurking," said old man Bransome. "He's run off to save that great big skin of his. He ain't bright, but he's got sense enough to do that."

Elk McMany looked mad and puffed out his chest. "You say another word like that, and I'll have the law on you. It is against the law to go around making unfounded charges, ain't it, sheriff?"

"It sure God is, Elk," the sheriff said and looked fiercely at old man Bransome.

"Well, then!" said Elk.

But three days passed, and Moose didn't show up.

I stopped in at the store and found Lula Mae looking worried.

"What's the matter?"

"I'm troubled about poor Moose," she said.

"About Moose? What about that poor little Sara Sanders whose neck he twisted?"

"She's going to get all right," said Lula Mae. "The doctor says so. But I can't help thinking about poor Moose hiding somewhere, scared to death, hungry, not really knowing what he's done."

"They're going to get the bloodhounds out after him, Daddy says."

Lula Mae froze and stared at me. "No," she sort of whispered. "No."

"Why not? He's dangerous. They can't let him just run around loose choking people. They'll shoot him if he tries to run."

"Shoot him?"

"Yes. Daddy heard them say so."

"Oh, he didn't mean to do anything," she said, her eyes filling up with tears. "Don't you remember that kitten years ago? Moose didn't even know he was hurting it. He just gets started on something like that and can't stop."

"They're getting the dogs out first thing in the morning," I said. "Elk raised Cain about it, and the sheriff wasn't eager. But Daddy says the police in the state capital are making them. I wonder where Moose could be hiding out?"

Lula Mae didn't say anything. She just stood there, thinking, as if I wasn't anywhere around.

"Lula Mae!" I said. "Are you off in a daze? I asked where you thought Moose might be hiding. Did he ever talk about any favorite hiding place of his? A cave, or something?"

Suddenly she seemed to snap back to being with me in the store. "Since Sara's going to get all right," she said, "they can't really do much to Moose if they do catch him. They can't shoot him! They can't!"

"Daddy says they ought to put him away somewhere," I said. "But I guess old Elk McMany can buy him out of 'most anything with that oil money."

"Maybe you're right," Lula Mae said, and then once again she seemed to go off into a kind of trance. She stood there a moment, not seeing me, and then she turned and walked back to the dingy little office where old man Bransome sleeps with his feet upon his roll-top desk.

So I left the store, worried. Lula Mae was always so close to me, so interested in what I had to say and do. This was the first time I ever felt she wasn't really with me, was far off somewhere else with thoughts she wasn't sharing.

When Daddy got home from work, it was twilight, much later than he usually came, and he was worried. He sort of half said hello to Mother, and then he got me off on a corner of the porch while she was fixing supper.

He looked me straight in the eye. "Have you seen Lula Mae this afternoon, Bo?"

His manner upset me, and from the look in his eyes I knew that something was wrong. "Yes, sir," I said. "I dropped in at Bransome's store on the way home from school and had a talk with her. Why?"

"She's gone," he said. "Disappeared, vanished."

I didn't know what to say, for suddenly far down inside me something knew exactly where Lula Mae was, at least, what she was trying to do, even if I didn't know the rightful place. But I didn't want to say so to Daddy. Somehow I didn't think he wanted to hear what he called my "uninformed guesses." So I just stood there silent, trying not to meet his eyes.

"Old man Bransome said he saw her talking to you just after dinner time. Is that true?"

"Yes, sir."

"Then, he said, she came back into his office all excited but trying to hide it. She blurted out something about her mother being sick and needing her and asked for the rest of the day off. Bransome said he wasn't surprised at her mother's being sick—she is every morning. But what did make him wonder was that it was the first time in his life he ever suspected Lula Mae of not telling the truth. She was so red-faced and breathless and wouldn't look him in the eye."

He stopped and stared at me, as if waiting for me to say something. But I didn't. I just stood there racking my brains for some sort of hint as to *where* Moose McMany would be hiding out.

At last Daddy spoke again. "So around five o'clock old man Bransome went by to see Sookie Persons, pretending to be asking about her health but really troubled about the way Lula Mae had acted. He found Sookie, all right. But she wasn't sick. She had a big bottle of Virginia Dare blackberry wine on the table and was singing hymns at the top of her voice. She didn't know anything about Lula Mae's asking off and thought she was still at the store."

Daddy paused again. Again, I didn't say anything. So he took me by the shoulder—I could feel his fingers biting into me.

"I have a feeling this business of Lula Mae's got something to do with that goddamned Moose. Do you know anything about it, Bo?"

"No, sir," I answered, but I could hear my voice, and I wouldn't have believed me.

"What did you and Lula Mae talk about?"

I looked at him straight. Like Lula Mae, I wasn't any good at lying. So I said just one word. "Moose."

"What about Moose?"

So I told him, told about how Lula Mae was afraid for Moose, how I'd told her about the dogs, and how if he ran they'd shoot him. Finally, I said, "I think she's gone hunting for Moose. Just to protect him. She believes he'll come back peaceably if she's gentle with him. The men with the guns and the dogs—they won't be gentle. She thinks they'll scare Moose, and he'll run or turn around and fight and get himself killed. She can't stand anything being hurt."

"Great God!" exclaimed Daddy, letting go my shoulder. "I guessed as much, but I just couldn't believe what I'd guessed. That Moose is a giant and a crazy man. He'll kill Lula Mae."

"I'm not so sure," I said. "He quit swinging that kitten when she asked him."

"This is more serious than any kitten.—Look here, Bo, have you got any idea where Moose might be hiding out?"

"No, sir. Not exactly, that is. I've seen him lumbering around on the hill near the millpond, the one with a lot of caves. But I just don't know."

So, instead of waiting for morning, the men with the guns and dogs started out that night. I could hear them leaving when Mother and I were sitting at the supper table. Daddy had gone with them. I could hear the kind of excited baying that hounds do when they're on the scent, excited and confused and yet somehow terrifying, especially if you hear them and know they're looking for you. I wondered if Moose could hear them, scrunched up in one of those caves near the millpond, the drool running down his chin and his big hands clenching and unclenching. And Lula Mae? I tried to wipe that picture out of my mind.

I didn't sleep much that night, for off and on I could hear the dogs. One time they came from over near the millpond; another, they seemed somehow to have gotten around to the other side of town where the woods are thickest. That baying shifted like some sort of fox-fire dancing around in the darkness.

And then it was morning.

I got up and looked out of my bedroom window because I could hear a kind of rumpus beginning in the direction of Bransome's store. Sure enough, I could see a huddle of people there, wavering like the reflection on a pool in the gray morning light.

I pulled on a pair of pants over my pajamas and ran.

There must have been twenty people there, and what they were wearing would have made me laugh at any other time. Mrs. Jackson, who always gives herself such airs, was wrapped in an old flannel bathrobe with her hair up tight in curling rags. Old man Robinson had come without his teeth, and his face looked sort of caved in.

But they weren't funny. It gives you a real uneasy feeling to see your friends and neighbors turn into a mob. Because that's what they were. Their faces that I knew so well looked strange, almost like foreigners. They were crowding around the store, and some of them were chanting, in a breathy kind of voice, "Lynching's too good for him!" Others were answering with "Tie him to a tree and pour kerosene on him!"

And there, slumped on the steps, was Moose.

His clothes were all torn and dirty, and his one bare foot was covered with blood where he'd cut it on stones and briars. His face was a mass of scratches as if a tiger had raked its claws across him. But it was his eyes that troubled me most. They didn't look afraid or mad, just surprised, as if he couldn't understand why all these people were yelling at him and threatening him. He seemed to be mumbling something over and over again.

I eased around the crowd and somehow managed to come up to Moose from behind. And then I heard what it was he kept repeating.

"She told me to come in and you wouldn't do me no harm. She told me to come in and you wouldn't do me no harm." Over and over he said it, and stared, unbelieving, at the many-eyed, many-fisted beast that threatened him.

Just then the sheriff and Elk McMany came up at a trot, and the crowd parted to let them through. I backed up against the wall of the store to be out of the way. The sheriff and Elk leaned down to hear what Moose was saying. Then Elk whispered something to the sheriff, fast and sharp.

The sheriff stood on the bottom step and raised his hand for silence.

"Now, you good people, there ain't nothing to get worked up about. Moose here has just told me that he come in of his own free will to give himself up—not that he admits to being guilty of anything—that ain't been proved yet—but just because he heard we were out looking for him."

At that moment the men with the dogs straining at the leashes came roaring down the street. I could see Daddy among them, his face not showing how he felt. When they saw the sheriff and Moose, they stopped and began getting the dogs to quiet down. The crowd in front of the store turned to watch them, and the sheriff and Elk got Moose by the arms and led him off, while everybody was looking the other way.

Daddy saw me on the porch and came over to me.

"Is she back yet?" he demanded

"Who?" I asked, not wanting to hear the rest of what was coming.

"Lula Mae," he said sharply. "Is she back yet?"

"I don't know. I ain't seen her."

He grabbed me by the arm and almost dragged me down the dirt street to the Persons' house. It was all dark, not a sign of life. We went up the overgrown walk lined with bottles stuck into the ground to make a border. Daddy pounded on the door. At first no one answered. Then we could hear a kind of stirring and groaning. Next the door eased open a crack, and I could see Mrs. Persons' eye, bloodshot and half-shut.

"What you want?" she demanded thickly.

"Has Lula Mae come home yet?" Daddy said, and his tone stirred even the dazed Mrs. Persons to respect.

"Wait a minute," she said and disappeared.

I could hear her feet slurring their way down the hall. After a minute she came back.

"Her bed ain't been slept in," she said. Then she let out a piercing wail. "Oh, my little daughter! Oh, what have they done to her?"

"Shut up, Sookie!" Daddy's voice cut through the wailing like a knife. "Go get yourself dressed and halfway sober. Lula Mae is still missing."

But Lula Mae came home. It was about three hours later, and I saw her dragging herself up her front steps. If anything, she looked worse than Moose did. Her hair was matted with clay, her face and arms were all bruised and scratched, and her clothes were torn half off her. She went inside and shut the door, leaving the little crowd that had followed her down the street standing there without any answers to their questions.

In a few minutes I saw Elk McMany hurrying down the street. He pushed through the crowd and went inside the Persons' house. He stayed there quite a while, and when at last he came out, he paused on the porch.

"Everything's all right, folks," he said, and if I'd shut my eyes I'd have thought it was Preacher Rankin talking. "I have just talked to Miss Lula Mae Persons, and I have the whole story, straight from her own lips. Hearing of the false gossip about my son and knowing that he would be the last person on earth to choke anybody, she went out to find him and persuade him to return and prove that all the talk about him was lies. She found him, she tells me, in a cave above the millpond. Here it is that he goes often to cook weenies and to be close to nature. He was appalled when he heard the charges being made, and the two of them started back to town. But Lula Mae's foot slipped, and she fell down a steep part of the hill. She was, I am sorry to say, knocked unconscious. But my son, disregarding his own safety, climbed down and rescued her." Here Elk sounded like he was finishing the "Benediction." "And that, my friends, is the whole story."

"What took her so long to get here, then?" called out a voice. "Moose came in a long time before she did."

Other voices joined in, demanding an answer.

Elk cleared his throat. "Friends, my boy carried her for the better part of two miles. Then his strength gave out. So he came in to get help. But you—"And here Elk looked like the Angel of God. "But you were so eager to lynch him that you didn't give him a chance to talk. Good day, friends."

Elk came down the walk, brushing his way through the crowd, and went on home, his blue serge suit shining at the elbows in the morning sun.

A few minutes later the crowd scattered, and I went home. But I sat on my front steps where I had a good view of the Persons' house.

As soon as the street was clear, Mrs. Persons came out and made a beeline for Bransome's store. She disappeared inside, and in about ten minutes she came out with a big paper bag in her arms. She hurried back to her house and slammed the door behind her.

That night we could hear her singing hymns at the top of her voice until about three o'clock.

The next day was Saturday, so I went over to Lula Mae's in the morning and whistled outside her window. I'd found out that she hadn't gone to Bransome's store to work, and I was fairly sure she was at home. But no matter how loud I whistled our mockingbird whistle, she didn't come.

Mrs. Persons kept up her singing both night and day until about Tuesday, but Lula Mae never came out.

Tuesday Jim Sanders drove up to the store in a brand-new Ford and said that his little girl was getting along fine after her "fall."

"Fell right out of a tree, she says, and landed *kerplump* on her head," Jim said. "Lucky she wasn't hurt worse."

Somehow that still didn't explain how her neck got all those blue bruises. But if Jim was satisfied, it seemed everybody else was. Especially Elk McMany. Though he wasn't there to show it. He was off with his family to Louisiana to look over his oil properties.

Finally Lula Mae came out of the house. But when I dropped in at Bransome's store after school, she was real quiet. She wouldn't say anything about Moose or how she got so bunged up except, "It wasn't poor Moose's fault. He just gets excited and can't stop what he's started. I don't blame him."

But she seemed real far off from me, farther off than she had that day I'd told her about the men and the dogs going after Moose. It was like she was behind a thick glass screen. I could see her, but somehow I couldn't touch her. And when she finished work at the store she hurried home and stayed inside there until she had to go to work again.

I didn't see her—except glimpses as she went to and from the store —for several months.

And then the talk started.

Mother was having the Methodist Ladies Auxiliary in for a Bible study meeting one afternoon. I was hanging around in the hall waiting for some of the leftover refreshments and sort of half-hearing Mrs. Jim Sanders teaching the lesson about "Suffer the little children to come unto me." When she finished and the ladies started in on the chicken salad sandwiches and Russian tea, Mrs. Jackson let out one of her high-toned giggles and said, "Our text seems peculiarly fitting for this neighborhood, don't it, Maria?"

"What do you mean?" asked Mrs. Nealey.

"Well, it certainly looks like children—or, at least, *a* child—is coming unto somebody in this neighborhood soon."

"Oh?" said Mrs. Nealey. "Who?"

And then Mrs. Jackson whispered, and there was a lot of oohing and ahing.

"What can you expect with a mother like that?" said Mrs. Sanders righteously.

It was soon after this that Lula Mae quit working at the store and never came out of the house at all. And then Elk McMany paid Mrs. Persons another visit. Thereafter, Mrs. Persons had a standing order at Bransome's store, and the delivery boy carried it to her in a big paper bag every morning right after breakfast. Mrs. Persons' hymn-singing reached new heights and stayed there. She kept it up until long after she could carry a tune. Usually she trailed off into silence around four in the morning.

I wondered how Lula Mae could put up with it. But I never found out because she stayed inside the house all the time now.

One morning about eleven o'clock we heard a shrill screaming from the Persons' house. It was, I remember now, Thanksgiving. Mrs. Persons had varied her hymns the night before with an occasional rendition of "Gobble, Gobble, Gobble, Fat Turkeys Are We," a song Lula Mae and I had learned in grammar school.

But now Mrs. Persons wasn't singing. She was screaming.

Daddy ran down the street, with me following.

Mrs. Persons was standing on the porch, leaning really, for she was hanging onto a spindly column, and screaming and screaming. She had on an old Japanese kimono and a boudoir cap, and she looked horrible.

Daddy ran up the steps and grabbed her and shook her.

"What is it, Sookie?" he yelled. "What is it?"

She toppled against him and sobbed. "I should have spent the money for that awful quack doctor. That's what Elk gave it to her for. I should have!"

Daddy let her sink back against the column and went into the house. I went, too. It was dark and cluttered and hadn't been swept in months. But we found our way to Lula Mae's room.

She was lying on the bed. I try not to remember how she looked.

Daddy picked up a piece of paper from the bedside table and read it. Then he turned and looked down at Lula Mae.

He didn't seem to notice when I took the paper from his hand.

I read it. "I have ate the rat poison," it said. "God have mercy on my soul."

I don't like to think of Lula Mae dying. I can't think of her as dead.

GEORGE H. LYNN, twenty-five, is originally from Spartanburg. This Limestone College graduate is now engaged in earning his Master of Fine Arts degree from the University of North Carolina at Greensboro. Two of Mr. Lynn's one-act plays were produced at Limestone College. His other credits include both fiction and poetry, published in *The Lantern, The Candelabra,* and *The Review of College Poetry.* "Forests of the Night," as presented here, is a segment from Mr. Lynn's novel by that same title, still in progress.

Forests of the Night

The winter sun shone cold on stone. Staley Barnes breathed frost and smoke and stretched his denim flank across a frozen rock to wait.

"I'm a lizard," he thought. "I'm a black lizard monster sunning myself in the white glare of winter. My blood is cold, and my body stiff; I will remain here upon the firmness of this rock until the spring thaw."

Bright rays glinted off of the mirror sunglasses that Stanley wore. The flashes of white and silver attracted curious stares from other students passing across the Brunswick College campus. Staley's shiny black leather motorcycle jacket reflected sparks as he shifted his weight slightly, the many buttons and zippers glittering chromely in the sunlight. Staley felt his flank growing numb with the cold and blending into the gritty fabric of stone.

"I can't move. I'm like solid death, like rock. I have nothing to consider, nothing to decide."

His body began to shake in small silent shudders.

"Tiger! Tiger! burning bright," he whispered aloud. There was a clear urgency in his chant, "Tiger! Tiger! burning bright, in the forests of the night; Tiger, Tiger . . ."

His eyes watched the moving students crossing the space between himself and Main Building. He moved his head into the sun, knowing this movement would send the reflections to the passers-by. He imagined these extensions to be his lizard tongue flicking out, testing his environment.

"Look . . . there's Staley Barnes . . . over there, sitting on the gym steps. He must be freezing."

"Yeah, O. K. . . . I see 'em. He's showing his ass as usual. He'd sit up there through a blizzard to get a few stares. He's the damnedest egomaniac I've ever seen. The guy's nuts."

Yes . . . I guess you're right," she said. There was a trace of sadness in her voice. Alice Williams was an impressionable girl. Her opinions always tottered on a fence edge, waiting for some dependable authority to push them off, one way or another. It just depended upon whom she was with as to how she felt about things.

Today she walked with Oliver Byrd, president of Alpha Mu fraternity, a very influential student at Brunswick College, who also happened to detest Staley Barnes. Barnes was a strange but constant menace to Oliver. It seemed like Barnes was always getting in the way of everything.

Staley, intent on the moving refractions of light from the gleaming frozen fountain which stood in solid ice in the middle of college square, did not notice Oliver and Alice pass. Actually, he hardly ever noticed Oliver. He thought of him as a red-faced buffoon who sputtered when he talked and wasted money on fruity clothing.

After lunch, Oliver emerged from Main Building. Staley Barnes was still stretched out across the gym steps. Oliver had Alice with him, a couple of his Alpha Mu brothers, and Freda Munson, an attractive redhead that Oliver had been trying to screw for over a year without success. The project had become a mania. Freda, besides being a sexy, good-looking girl, was a talented artist and her paintings were well known all over town. If Oliver could somehow add her to his long list of conquests, he might also be considered vicariously aesthetic, a realm of affectation he had yet to squeeze into.

When Oliver saw Staley, he thought that was the perfect time to show up the hick and impress Freda. The group moved toward the gym at his suggestion.

Staley saw them coming, a mass of shadow emerging from the sun.

"Alert, Alert; bandits at twelve o'clock. Focke wulfs."

There was an electric hum as the glass dome swung around and brought the lethal twin fifties to bear upon the enemy. The wind howled through the small barrel openings in the plexiglass turret, and rippled the fur of Staley's flight jacket. His thumb tensed on the butterfly trigger . . . "steady . . ." No, today he was not the brave ball turret gunner; he was the reptile, the carrier of the fatal seed. "Tiger! Tiger! burning bright," he whispered. He flicked his tongue, luminous and bright, toward the intruders as a solemn warning.

"Well, if it isn't Brunswick's own Hell's Angel."

Oliver's crack lacked authority. As he had gotten near to the black form an odd feeling of weakness had crept up his legs and thighs, chilling his groin and constricting his throat. When he spoke, his voice came out in a girlish shriek.

Staley turned his head very slightly so that the offender could catch the distorted image of his own face in the mirror glasses. This unnerved Oliver more, and he did not like the fact that Staley had made no answer. Oliver felt one leg begin to quiver.

"Who are you supposed to be anyway? Marlon Brando or a delinquent Eskimo?"

Alice giggled and Freda smiled; both frat men snickered. This response made Oliver feel better. He stood firmer and leered a bit.

"I'm a lizard, a reptile."

"A liz . . . you're a what for cris' sake?"

More smiles and snickers, and pokes in fraternal ribs. Staley stood up, and they quieted and waited to see what the lizard would do. Staley stretched, forcing chilled blood into the vessels of his petrified limbs, then casually reached into one of the unzipped pockets of his motorcycle jacket. He withdrew his hand bringing out a slim rectangular object about seven inches in length. He held it up and it snapped with a sharp metal click. Staley's arm recoiled with the appearance of six inches of silver metal. Again the lizard shone in the sunlight with his polished steel. He turned the fine sharp blade over twice to admire the razor edge, and to allow for the full effect of its presence. Then he pointed the blade straight at Oliver's throat and descended three of the gym steps, stopping one step above the terrified student. Oliver took one panic-stricken step backward and almost fell. A cry of protest stuck in his throat and a sound between a whimper and a squeak emerged. Beneath his paralyzing fear he felt a queer sensual fascination.

"My great-great-grandfather was a thunder lizard. Before I saw light, he roamed the earth unafraid. Now I am descended from his blood and I, too, shall devour the flesh of my enemies."

The solemnity of Staley's voice hung in the air like an icicle. Oliver croaked like a frog. His eyes moved wildly to his friends and back to Staley, but he did not move his head lest the blade rip into the bare flesh of his throat.

Behind the mirror glasses Staley's eyes lost interest. Again his gaze was lost in the viscera of his own thigh. Deftly he clicked the blade shut with a movement of his palm against his leg, and brushed past the gaping prey. He crossed the campus without hearing Freda Munson's derisive laughter, or considering the damage he had achieved. The scene was lost to him three steps past Oliver.

He stopped at the art building and sat down on a short row of concrete steps. Now he was completely enveloped by shadow because the sun was obscured by the bulk of the huge brick building. His body shook from the cold. The chill had worked its way inside him.

"I am a lizard," he tried, "and it's all very natural." It wasn't working. "I am a lizard," he thought, "but I have this dark closet inside my head that's full of dead bodies and stinking skeletons. It smells of rot and cheap whiskey, and death. Sometimes I can hear my mother's voice yelling for Daddy to jam his foot in the casket crack." He heaved a long sigh.

"This thing . . . this . . . serpent is crushing my gut like ice. Dare I frame thy fearful symmetry . . . Tiger! Tiger!"

He stood up and looked out across the campus. The blurred edges of his peripheral vision channeled his sight into an unblurred squarish shape. He stretched one arm out as far as he could and flattened his palm against the air.

"This is a surface," he said, "a wall as solid as the stone which I sunned upon, or the case of electricity which hides my mind, or the years of acts before my birth, and behind this wall crouches the monster."

Staley dropped his arm and laughed. "I should have a peg leg made of bone," he thought. Then he turned and walked up the steps, affecting a limp and trying to look demonic. He entered the shaded building feeling very cold and alone. The names Jesus Christ, Captain Marvel, and John Milton kept popping through his mind.

Still standing on the gym steps, his muted rage boiling in bewilderment, Oliver had watched Staley raise and drop his arm. "He's crazy," Oliver thought, "the guy is really nuts." He watched the black figure disappear into the mysterious art building, and hated him.

TOM PARKS, thirty-two, worked his way through college as police reporter and later as the editor of daily and weekly newspapers. He eventually founded and published his own weekly before going into teaching. Mr. Parks has published two articles and several poems in smaller magazines and is the author of *The Theme Machine,* a college handbook for writing compositions. While teaching in colleges in Pennsylvania and Louisiana, he compiled and edited two volumes of student poetry. He is currently the English Consultant for South Carolina's Department of Education, where he serves as editor of *Horizon,* a quarterly publication for English teachers, and as the host of a monthly television program, "Spectrum," shown on the state's ETV network for English teachers throughout South Carolina.

Tiger, Tiger

Blackburn Swamp lay serene and golden under primordial moonlight, with teeming undercurrents of life hidden in its darkest reaches beneath the high night sky. A white dirt road coiled like a glowing serpent through the depths of the black timber until it looped around to the edge of a clearing where a house stood, solemn and shadowy with unpainted planks and deep dull windows.

Then there was the loud, rising scream, like an echo from antiquity, starting off low, so low that at first you couldn't be sure, then rising higher and higher in a rending jagged orange-colored arc of sound that ripped the darkness and soared over the looming treetops, splitting the muted hues of the night woods until it sank lower and lower and finally died in a gargled moan, as if soaked up by the dank dark floor of the swamp.

Inside the house, the boy stirred in his sleep and cried. He had always heard it this way at night, late at night in his dreams, years before he was old enough to know what it was. It had always been there, it seemed to him, even back before he could remember. There was no beginning to it.

"You all right, Cal?"

The boy sprang awake, tense and rigid.

"You been crying in your sleep," his mother said. "What's the matter? You all right?" She put her hand on his forehead.

He was all right, he told her, his eleven-year-old hairspring body beginning to loosen.

"But this time I heard it. I know I really heard it," he whispered intensely as he slid back down in bed.

"Go on back to sleep," she said. She said it in a different way than usual—not consoling or comforting him but in a balanced and even voice that made him sense the truth.

She heard it tonight, too, he knew. How many other times had she heard it, he wondered; how many other nights when she had told him it was just a bad dream? *There's not any tigers around here,* she would tell him. *They're in a country across the waters. I didn't hear anything. You've just been dreaming again. Go on back to sleep.*

And always, the next morning dawned new for the boy growing up in the South Carolina swamp, and the dreams of the night before seemed distant and somehow unreal, like a hazy memory. With his parents he was a creature of the sunlight and lived in it and by it on their bottom-land farm. And sunlight was not the place for tigers.

But this night, tonight, was different.

She has heard it, he knew. He knew. *There is a tiger.*

Cal eased out from under the quilts and stood listening at the door to their room.

"You ought to talk to him in the morning," he heard his mother say as she settled back down in their bed, making the springs squeak. "So he'll stop dreaming about it. You ought to talk to him."

"I'm leaving early for the mill," his father answered in a low voice that Cal could barely hear. "I'll talk to him when I get back."

Then, a little louder, his mother's voice: "And I intend to get after me some Negroes about it. I know they're the cause of it in the first place, scaring him to death with all their tales. I know they're the ones to blame, calling it a tiger. It's just a panther—them and their stories."

"A wildcat," his father answered so low that Cal could tell he was on the edge of sleep.

Later, just before Cal started to ease back into his room, his mother spoke again to the darkness. "It sounded like a woman," she said. "Just like a woman crying out from pain."

Then there was silence, and Cal slipped back to his bed.

Outside, Gypsy jumped up on the porch. Cal could hear her scratching fleas and then curling up to go back to sleep.

Then there was another sound, a small whimpering and shuffling sound, and he knew that the puppy had been following Gypsy and was trying to get up the high porch steps. He eased over to the outside door and opened it.

"Pat," he whispered. "Here, Pat, c'mon, puppy."

The puppy clambered up the last step and came waddling over to him, a frenzy of tail-wagging. Gypsy was coming, too, but Cal picked up the puppy and quietly pushed the door closed before she could get in. She whined outside a couple of times, then went back and curled up on the porch.

"Shhh," he calmed the squirming puppy as he crawled under the covers. He put it at the foot of the bed, but it came nuzzling and whimpering back to him. He held up the quilts and it crawled down to his side and lay still.

"I'll not have it," Cal's mother said the next morning when she came in to wake him and was surprised when the puppy stuck its head from beneath the cover. "You'll get fleas all over you, much less dirtying up the bedclothes. Wash up now and come on to breakfast."

Cal sat in the kitchen eating and wished he could have gone with his father. He wondered if his father took the long way. It was a winding dusty road that meandered through miles and miles of the golden autumn woods in the swampland, curving here to cross a creek and there to frame a field and on past to an occasional farmhouse. Along the way the road made a sharp curve and looped up to the group of Negro tarpaper shacks which everybody called "the settlement," but Cal knew of a shortcut through the woods behind his house that led across the footlog on Chaney Creek and straight to the Negro community.

"He's been gone too long for you to catch up with him," his mother said when he asked. "Besides, he won't be back until late," she added, clearing the table where he was finishing breakfast.

He took a thick slice of fried ham and a biscuit and went outside.

"And don't be feeding that to the dog," she called after him.

He squinted in the early morning sun, ready to ramble the woods with Gypsy. The puppy came trotting in its curious sideways gait around the corner of the house. He knelt down and watched it as it trotted into the tall grass, where its short legs completely lost pace and stumbled in all directions.

"Here, Pat," he called, adding a couple of whistles, and laughed as the fat little brown-and-tan beagle made a stumbling run in his direction. It was the last of six puppies Gypsy had given birth to two months ago. Cal had talked long and hard for his father not to give this one away like the others.

The puppy reached him and sat licking his fingers where he had held the piece of ham.

Cal looked up at the Saturday morning sun and down again at the puppy. He remembered the day it was born. Bummy-jaw Sawyer, a tall and gangly harmonica-playing Negro from the settlement, had come to their front porch and told them Gypsy had had her puppies during the night over at the settlement.

"Wonder why she had them there?" Cal's father had asked. "Wonder why not here around home."

"Don't know. Can't ever tell about dogs," Bummy-jaw had answered. "Somebody found her early this morning in the lean-to shed. Looks like pretty puppies, except one is a runt."

"Well I certainly don't want to fool with a litter of puppies," Cal had heard his father say. "Why don't you all just keep them?"

Cal could still remember the way he felt, looking up at Bummy-jaw's tall, grinning face and holding his breath.

"Maybe one or two," he had been relieved to hear the Negro man answer, "after they're weaned in a few weeks."

So in the meantime Gypsy and the puppies would have to be brought home.

"I'll bring 'em," Bummy-jaw had said, "to get first pick." Then he looked down at Cal. "You want to help me bring them?"

So off the two had gone that day, through the woods to the settlement, with Cal hurrying to keep up while Bummy-jaw took long ambling steps and played the harmonica all the way. It was then that Cal had learned of the shortcut to the Negro settlement, of the footlog across Chaney Creek. It was on a Saturday, like today.

I should have named you Runt, Cal thought as he sat there scratching the puppy's head in the morning sun.

He stood up and whistled for Gypsy. She came bounding around the corner to him.

"Let's go, Gypsy! Let's go, girl!" he clapped his hands and ran out of the yard toward the backwoods.

It was a balmy day, with not many leaves left on the trees—one of the aimless slow times when to Cal the whole world seemed to be basking in a lazy golden sunlight under the distant sky. Today he would go to the narrow point where the footlog crossed Chaney Creek. The banks had caved in from a washout and willows were growing down next to the water, making a swift narrow channel not over six feet wide for the water to gush through. It was a good place to make a paddle wheel out of palmetto leaves and twigs and set it turning in the edge of the water.

Gypsy ran along up ahead of him, crashing through the dry crackly leaves and undergrowth on first one side of the trail, then the other. If Pat were a little bigger, he told himself, he would have let him come. But he knew the short little legs wouldn't have lasted long. It was a day to drift around, mostly, he figured, without having to worry with things like little puppies that couldn't keep up.

"Come on, Gypsy," he called to the dog, who was sniffing around the edge of a hole.

He walked on through the thick timber, breaking into a playful run at times with Gypsy until finally he came to the narrow place at the creek where the willows grew. The water was swift here and gurgled among the willow roots and branches that tangled in a maze along the edge. Up where the creekbed first narrowed, a huge tree which had washed out of the crumbling banks years before was stuck end to end across the expanse of the water, making a footlog from one side to the other.

The gurgling of the water as it rippled through the narrow chute in the willow-laced bed was pleasant to Cal, peaceful sounding. He knelt by the edge and slowly dragged his hand through the water, feeling the ripples and bubbles tingle against his palm. It was cold. He could feel the warm sun basking his neck and back, and he seemed strangely in the middle of things: the rushing water too cold, the beaming sun too warm, but both blending into just the right combination inside him. He gave in to a lazy feeling that possessed him and didn't move from where he knelt, blending into the silent scene whose only sound was the light gurgling voice of the water among the willows. His eyes drooped and soon became so nearly closed that only a few lazy slivers of golden light squeezed beneath his eyelids. He was somewhere between sleeping and waking, drowsing there with his hand trailing in the water and his back to the sun, belonging to no place, no time.

His thoughts drifted slowly away from the scene before him, from the time and place where he knelt, and began forming other times and places of their own. He dreamed he was walking in the woods again, this time near home where he knew every trail, every tree. Gypsy and Pat both were with him, and he had to keep his eye on the puppy because it was too little to keep up and might get lost. Then Gypsy bounded on ahead, leaving him and the puppy, and wouldn't come back, wouldn't obey when he called out to her. She ran on far ahead, out of sight, and he felt lost because she wouldn't come back. Then he remembered the puppy and turned to see it run away in the opposite direction, and he chased after it. "Pat!" he was calling, "Pat!" running through the woods after it, but it was always just out of sight ahead of him. Then he was in a darkening part of the swamp where he hadn't been before, and he saw Pat lying asleep under a little brown bush. When he reached down, the puppy snarled at him and snapped back with its needlelike teeth, and then the bush moved and he saw that it was the tiger itself, rising higher and higher and bigger as it turned on him and blotted out the light, enveloping the puppy in its shadow and looming over him where he stood before it, dwarfed and stricken. Then he was running through the swamp, crashing through the limbs and underbrush, trying to stay in the light before the looming shadow behind caught and engulfed him.

His eyes snapped open. He was instantly awake. The crashing of the underbrush in his dream was real now and coming from behind him in the timber, heading straight to where he knelt at the creek's edge. Something—something big—was crashing through the woods and was right upon him, charging right toward the bank where he knelt. He grabbed Gypsy and froze, staring up.

The figure shot out of the weeds and brush in a flurry of leaves and dry twigs and soared over the boy's head onto the footlog, sprawling into a grotesque heap at the water's edge on the other side, with arms flailing wildly in all directions. Sprays of mud and water exploded from the impact, and Cal was peppered where he sat, frozen, paralyzed, with eyes staring wide at what he saw.

It was Bummy-jaw, splotched now with mud and caked leaves and water from where he landed at the edge of the creek. Cal blinked, not sure. He had never seen the man look so wild, so different.

"Bummy-jaw?" he called, but it came out only a whisper.

The man had scrambled up now and was clambering up the bank but slipped in his own covering of slick mud and water and went sliding back down to the water's edge, where he immediately clawed for another foothold, his arms flailing the air wildly.

"Bummy-jaw!" Cal called louder this time.

The man jerked around at the sound, slipping again and losing his foothold.

"Tiger!" he yelled. "Tiger!" And then he reached the top of the bank. "Tiger caught in the shed. We got him caught in the lean-to shed!"

The boy jumped up, his mouth hanging open and his eyes staring at the man blankly.

"Your father with you?" Bummy-jaw asked and jerked his head up and down the river, searching.

"No. I'm by myself," the boy answered. "The tiger's caught?" he asked barely loud enough to hear himself, his mouth still hanging open and his eyes still staring.

"It got trapped hunting chickens last night; we heard it in there this morning. We got to get a gun," the man yelled over his shoulder as he tore off through the woods towards Cal's home. He vanished into the trees, and Cal could hear the sound of him breaking through the limbs and brush. Finally he was out of hearing.

The boy turned slowly and looked in the direction of the settlement, as if he might see a huge dark shadow looming over it. He stood there transfixed, staring at the woods.

The tiger, caught? He didn't understand, it didn't make sense or wasn't right somehow. He couldn't focus his mind on anything; it was all too fast and too blurred to catch onto.

Gypsy reared up onto his side with her front paws touching his belt. He looked down silently into her eyes. She whined softly up at him, and it brought things back into place, back into focus.

He looked up at the sun. It seemed high and weak, but it was still warm and golden. *It's not the tiger they've caught.* A stray wildcat, maybe, but not the tiger, not in the open sunlight like this now.

I will see it for myself, while it's daylight, he thought.

He took off through the trees, dodging through the undergrowth towards the settlement. Gypsy chased behind him, barking at his heels, and then ran past him through the woods, waiting for him to catch up. Soon he was panting, out of breath, stumbling time after time, but he kept on. The dog had stopped barking and ran beside him, intent and quiet. He began taking deep rattling breaths as he ran on, his heart pounding and his legs flying through the underbrush, over logs and down into gullies and up again without slowing. Once he tripped over his own feet and went stumbling in a long aimless fall that piled him on his back against the foot of a sycamore sapling, which rained down a scattering of its last yellow leaves. For a second he lay there on his back, exhausted beyond reason and breathing heavily. But before the exhaustion could strangle him, he scrambled up and was off again. He had to get there to see, before it was all over, before it might end, before someone could tell him he was forbidden to look at it.

As he ran he knew it might not be there for long, might be gone before he got there, and the thought made him keep on at his breakneck run toward the settlement, even when his breath and his body passed out of consciousness. He couldn't breathe fast enough, but he didn't know it or didn't care as he ran on.

How had it trapped itself there? He pictured the shed and knew it wouldn't hold for long. It was where they had found Gypsy when she had her puppies. He could picture the tabletop door hanging on its haywire hinges, loose and flimsy like the shed itself, just a lean-to against the barn, built of leftover things never meant to be part of any prison. The whole thing quivered and shook and rattled, he imagined, with every breath of the thing that was caught inside it now. He pictured it crouching there in the darkness of the shed, its gaping red mouth and burning, staring eyes turned upon him from where it loomed in the dark of some deep hidden lair which nobody could find but which he kept stumbling into in his dreams.

He ran on, not realizing he had stopped breathing and not feeling the scratches and whiplashes from the underbrush or the leaves and mud smeared on his knees and elbows where he had stumbled and sprawled out on the floor of the swamp.

Then he broke loudly through the underbrush and out into the clearing at the edge of the settlement. He froze there for a minute staring, his shoulders heaving and his breath fighting loudly for more air, fighting in hoarse rasping gulps.

There were only two people he saw, a woman at a window in one of the shacks and an old man standing at the foot of a live oak in the middle of the clearing not far from him, with one hand on a low branch of the tree and the other grasping a hoe. He saw nobody else, and he and the old man stood staring at each other across the clearing.

Then he heard it and jerked his head toward the shed. It was a high-pitched wail, cut short suddenly when the cat hit against the loose door, trying to force an opening.

He took a step back.

Again the cat hit, and the door shook on its loose moorings.

He tried to take a deep breath, but it wouldn't catch and came gasping out again for more air, still gulping desperately. It flashed to his mind suddenly that his shoulders were heaving terribly and his breaths weren't big enough or something, coming in loud deep rasping sounds.

He stepped back, trying to hold.

Then there was another loud wail from the shed and another rattling crash as the door tore loose from its bottom hinge and hung at a sloping angle which left a gaping dark hole at the bottom.

He heard the woman in the shack scream. The cat burst through the bottom opening and crouched there as if frozen into place, its lips curled back in a low growl.

It was little. He couldn't get over how little it was. How very small it looked, crouched there in a tight snarling bundle of tawny fur and fangs. *What is it?* he wondered, staring incredulously at it where it seemed frozen before him into a molded lump of brindled clay in the weak sunlight.

Then he saw its head turn slowly, ever so slowly, taking in all that lay before it, including him standing there near the edge of the swamp. For a minute it seemed to him that its head froze and its eyes were staring directly into him, forcing him to stare back, unable to break away. Once more he gulped for breath, but this time he couldn't find it, it couldn't break loose again and was caught up inside him, clawing at his insides to get free.

Then he saw the staring, silent eyes of the cat turn orange and golden like the waning sun and grow bigger and bigger until they filled everything; the whole scene seemed bathed in a heavy amber light as he staggered backward. Just before he fell he saw the old man rush forward with the hoe drawn high over his head, saw the blade flash down and the cat burst away in a furious cry of pain while the old man ran backward and stumbled and fell. He saw Gypsy hurl herself at the tawny bleeding figure of the cat and then melt together with it into a rolling fighting ball of feet and fur and fangs, growling and groaning and crying in fury. Then, just on the edge of thought, just before it engulfed him, he heard the dog cry out, painfully and in agony.

Gypsy's dead, he thought, and fell headlong into a big golden whirlwind of spinning lights that grew dark and smothered him.

"Never mind. Never mind," somebody's voice awoke him. He was surprised to see it was his mother. Then Bummy-jaw was there, and some of the other Negroes, crowding around the bed in the tarpaper shack.

"Son? Son, are you all right now?" his mother bent down, pale and worried.

"Is Gypsy dead?" But he was too weak; they didn't understand him. He said it again, louder.

"Is Gypsy dead?"

Bummy-jaw knelt down beside the bed.

"You know," he said, "she finished off that tiger all right. We found it dead at the edge of the swamp. It couldn't crawl any further."

"Is Gypsy all right?"

"She was hurt too much," Bummy-jaw answered, and put his hand on the boy's arm. "Gypsy's dead."

Cal sat up. He felt empty and weak and wished he could be alone and cry or go back to sleep or something, but they were there. He stared at them blankly.

"You feel like trying to make it home now?" his mother asked.

They carried him home and put him to bed, and they put the puppy on the bed with him. Then his father came back, and Cal lay listening to them as they sat on the porch and told the whole story to his father, some parts over and over.

"Did you know—"

"The hoe cut it deep just behind its shoulder."

"It saw me just before the hoe hit it."

"And then the dog."

"And did you know—"

"What did it do to the dog?"

"Had one of her eyes out, stomach ripped open, neck and ears clawed bad."

"Mostly bled to death."

"Did you know she'd been nursing young?"

"No, I mean the cat. The cat."

"The dog, too. That's something."

"Yeah, but I mean the cat. She'd been nursing young ones. Not over a month ago."

Inside, Cal heard their voices drift away and blend together in the late evening air as sleep returned to him. The puppy stretched lazily against his arm and yawned, and Cal snuggled under the covers, watching the weakening orange bands of waning sunlight on the walls gradually lose focus and become blurred. The voices on the porch became more muted, and the blurred bands of sunlight turned to gray as he and the puppy slept.

When he awoke it was late in the night, with everything still and quiet and his parents sleeping. What had awakened him? He lay there, tense and listening.

Then he heard it. It started low and somewhat off to the north, so low that at first he wasn't sure. Then it started rising higher and higher in a thin clear whine, not as loud as before and not as long.

He knew. He sat up in bed, listening. Again it came, rising higher this time, an arching thin wail that slit the darkness.

Then something moved at his elbow. It was the puppy, sitting up, its ears cocked. It bounded off the bed in a tumbling jump and ran to the window. Cal could see it there in the moonlight, reared up with its front paws on the window ledge, its body taut and listening.

He eased out of bed and knelt beside it.

"Pat," he whispered, and held him up at the window. "Pat." He could feel the tense little brown-and-tan body quiver in his arms as the puppy gazed unblinking out into the night.

ROBERT M. JOHNSON has designs of becoming a novelist, though at the time of this writing his publishing had been restricted to the University of South Carolina literary magazine. He has written poetry, but most of his efforts have been in prose. For the past two years he has written short stories emphasizing themes of alienation, the search for alternative life styles, random violence, loneliness, and sense experience. As a result of his interest in surrealism, his stories rely greatly on imagery. A native of Washington, D.C., Mr. Johnson is presently attending the University of South Carolina, following two years of travel in this country and an extended residence in New York's East Village.

The Man with the Cane

The early morning light was a pleasant companion with him on the balcony. The yellow shafts of warmth soothed the harshness of the street's grimy stone buildings, making it a suitable moment to sip coffee.

As he drank he gently leafed through the pages of a local tabloid looking for articles of interest. Though he didn't expect to find much in the provincial newsletter, he went through the motions anyway.

His mornings on the balcony had become his last retreat—his last hope for sanity and peace of mind in a life that had become increasingly unbearable. For this reason he had reduced himself to clutching to a daily pattern of pretending grace and enjoyment.

From his position above the street he could watch all of the morning traffic come by, catch the excited voices of the local vendors, and maybe even see an oddity or two. . . .

Still, he recognized it as nothing more than a local anesthetic for the piteous cries of his wife, Edna.

This morning he thought that the street's activity was beginning a bit early. Carts of vegetables and produce were rolled out into the alleyways a shade before seven-thirty as the trucks that bore crates of squawking chickens and ducks rumbled along the pavement into position. Before long, the dark-faced women would come out with their homemade fabrics, and then a bit later the men in the coal trucks would come choking the whole lane in their black sooty clouds.

With his experienced eye he looked the familiar situation over quickly and it seemed as if nothing would change—but then he came upon something most unusual. A dark-dressed figure was making its way down the street. From the cut of his clothes he seemed to be a professional man and he was wearing a dark fedora as most of those gentlemen did, but what was most striking about the individual was his gait—he was limping. He was a cripple.

As he watched the figure he became more and more interested. It was the cripple's left leg that was lame and he supported himself with a rather stout brass-tipped cane. From the balcony he could almost feel the man's ancient pain as the useless limb stiffened, buckled, and dragged itself behind.

Curious about the man with the cane, he edged his chair closer to the railing for a better view.

He watched the gentleman as he struggled along the street, stopping occasionally at stalls to look over the merchandise. From the balcony it seemed as if the cripple was unaccustomed to the district and was merely browsing through the shops with the curiosity of a tourist.

The man with the cane paused at one stall and bought a bag of fruit. From the balcony it seemed as if he were looking about him protectively, as an animal might over its kill, before he began to eat.

Musing over the gentleman lead him to think of his wife Edna and their life since her accident. It seemed, as her strength had failed, so had her confidence in him. Now she had become a suspicious and unbearable shrew.

And as if to affirm his thoughts her whining voice called to him.

"John, what are you doing?"

"I'm out on the balcony, dear."

He prayed that she would stay behind the French doors.

"John, when will you take me for my walk?"

"It's too early, dear. Wait until the traffic isn't as busy."

He dreaded the thought of wheeling her about in her wheelchair. Not only did he have to talk with her, but he had to defend her from all of the imagined slights that people dealt her as well.

"John, will you come in and talk to me?"

"Dear, there will be plenty of time for that today. Please, just let me finish my coffee, will you?"

She quieted for a moment and then resumed the conversation.

"Are you watching the people today?"

"Yes, you know that I always do."

"Do you see any pretty girls out there today?"

The way she said it was meant to make him feel guilty. She wanted to persecute him even for his fantasies and he knew it.

He wanted to say that he was watching beautiful girls. He wished he could tell her there were many beautiful girls and he was violating every one of them with his eyes, but even she knew that the only women that ever came on the street were fat and coarse.

It was then that his eyes again came upon the man with the cane; he had paused by a newsstand and was looking through some magazines.

"No, dear, there aren't any girls out on the street—except the usual."

"Why don't you come in then?"

The gentleman paused from his magazine and as if he could sense John's thoughts he looked up towards the balcony.

"I'm watching somebody."

He could hear her pause in doubt and ask timidly, "Who is it?"

The man with the cane dropped his readings and struggled down the street towards him. His face was looking up at him the whole while, and as he brought his burden of pain closer and closer John could feel himself beginning to sweat.

"Who is it, John?", she demanded again.

"A man with a cane, Edna."

"What is he doing?"

"He's limping about the street."

He had spoken to her in the wrong tone and he knew that she understood what he was thinking, but in the midst of his compulsion he had been helpless.

"John, must you always be so cruel," she whimpered.

By now the cripple was right below the balcony and supporting himself heavily on his stick he peered up.

John looked down at him and tried to speak casually.

"Hello. How are you this morning?"

The gentleman replied and doffed his hat in a polite gesture, yet he refused to move.

"John? Who are you speaking to?"

"The man with the cane, dear."

"Will you help me out, John?"

"If you wish, dear."

Excusing himself before the gentleman with the cane he walked inside to his wife. She was still in her bedclothes and her face was pale from a painful night.

Taking her in his arms he placed her in her wooden wheelchair. Her skin, which once was so soft and beautiful, had become scaly and he could feel the hair on her legs.

"Would you like a comforter, dear?"

"No, John. Please take me out on the balcony."

Slowly he pushed her chair to the balcony. Outside, they found that the cripple was still standing below.

Edna immediately recognized his presence and nodded demurely to him,

"Good morning."

Once again the man tipped his hat, but he still didn't move. John, wondering about the strange creature, said,

"Would you care to join us on the balcony?"

The man glanced sharply up at him and then tapped the side of his damaged leg with the cane and mumbled, "No, I'm a cripple."

Edna looked angrily at John and bent over towards the gentleman.

"Has my husband insulted you?"

The cripple laughed a self-abasing laugh and shook his head.

"Oh, no, madam. No more than anyone else I meet on the street."

"I understand how you feel, I'm a cripple, too."

"Oh, really?"

"Yes, I was in a train-wreck and I can't walk."

"I was lamed by a streetcar."

John became apprehensive for he could envision how his wife would behave after the gentleman left, yet something inside him came out and forced him to speak.

"Surely you must come up. People will think it's rather strange like this."

The intruder wagged his finger accusingly at him and replied, "Ah, but isn't that what you really want?"

Before he could answer the cripple continued, "I saw you as you watched me walk this street. I saw the pity and condescension you gave me from your balcony. I know how you feel and I wanted to confront you with it all."

Edna said nothing but smiled enjoyably as John tried vainly to conceal what he had done.

"I'm sure I don't know what you mean—"

"Come now. You needn't pretend. I teach at the University and I know all of your reasons why. Much more, I imagine, than even you do. You feel that I am some sort of slimy lower-life form because of my injury, that you wouldn't get any closer to than with a microscope for fear of contamination. And from your point of view I'm sure that it's justified."

"I thought no such thing!" But John knew that he could only sound half-convincing before the combined scrutiny of the crippled man and Edna.

"Come now, sir. Your mind is filled with secret images of what my mangled limb looks like, and I bet that just once you would like to touch it and see if it feels the same as an ordinary leg might."

"You disgust me! If you are finished I wish you'd leave, before I call the police. I should be able to sit on my own balcony without being insulted."

"Oh, I'm leaving. And you are quite right that you should be able to sit in peace, but the problem is that you can't because you won't give peace to others. *This* you managed to do without even opening your mouth! May I congratulate you on your effectiveness and may I extend my sympathies to your wife, for having to put up with you and your oppressive nature. . . ."

Smiling again the man with the cane turned and limped away. Together, John and Edna sat for many moments watching him dragging his useless limb behind him until he was at last out of sight.

Edna broke the long silence in an intended voice.

"That cripple was pitiful."

John knew what she was thinking and of course she was forcing him to state himself.

"No, he was just a nasty old man."

Edna looked piercingly at him.

"Really, John?"

He glanced at her quickly and nodded and then turned away. He knew her thoughts too well.

She went on, "No, the problem is that you're normal and that's the only way that you can see things."

He paled at her words and wondered bitterly to himself, "Better that I should be a cripple?"

"Yet I suppose John, if we looked at it from another point of view—"

She paused in her thoughts to purse her lips.

"We'd find that you're a cripple, too, just as I am. Yes, just as I am!"

Her face filled with excitement and he stared once again from the balcony to all of the moving figures in the street . . . beneath him each of them seemed to pass with a limp and it was then that he understood what she had done.

HELEN BOLAND KING has published several historical and professional articles, poems, and a musical playlet in publications including *The State* newspaper, *The State Magazine,* a number of nationally known poetry periodicals, and internationally circulated magazines, such as *The Etude Music Magazine, The Grade Teacher,* and *The Instructor.* One of her historical articles, "The Old Columbia Theological Seminary," is listed in the bibliography for the restoration of Columbia's historic Ainsley Hall mansion. Poet Laureate Archibald Rutledge said that *Carolina Carols,* her first collection of poems, is "destined to become a permanent part of South Carolina's literary heritage." She has been the recipient of state and national literary prizes, including the grand prize in *The State-Quill* literary contest with her sonnet, "Barren Woman." She is a teacher in the Columbia Public Schools and is active in music circles of the capital city. "Christmas Under Lake Murray" first appeared in *Sandlapper, The Magazine of South Carolina.*

Christmas Under Lake Murray

At Christmas time I love to gaze out over the deep waters of Lake Murray in the heart of the Dutch Fork section of South Carolina, so-called because it is in the fork of the Broad and Saluda Rivers, and was mainly settled by German people, and was called Deutschland for their homeland. As I look over the still bosom of the lake I can see the reflection of Christmas tree lights from other cottages that dot the shore around our own lake home. I enjoy the informal neighborhood gatherings and, as we munch on Christmas goodies and listen to the hi-fis and televisions pouring out yuletide music, I sometimes feel apart from the group, as a spectator watching characters on a stage. Time magically turns backward in its flight and I am a little child again, and it is Christmas on my grandfather's farm, which is now completely inundated by the waters of Lake Murray.

Both my parents were natives of Dutch Fork so it was not unusual at Christmas time for them to load their children, themselves, and a pile of mysterious looking packages into our Maxwell or Model T and journey to my grandparents' for the holidays. Though the distance was not more than a hundred miles it took the best part of the day to make

the trip, for the roads at that time were quite a contrast to the maze
of superhighways that stretch hypnotically through the freshly carved
countryside.

My oldest brother, not yet a teen-ager, always had to sit in the front
seat with my father in order to assist with the removal of a tree limb
or a stray cow or pig that often blocked the road. Sometimes we had to
cross a high, precarious-looking bridge over a swift up-country river,
and Mama would have Papa stop the car and she would get out and
walk across the narrow bridge with the baby and anyone else whose
courage wavered. We often got lost on the unmarked roads, especially
if Papa had a mind to try a shortcut some well-meaning traveler had
told him about. We always carried a shovel in the car in case we got
stuck in the mud or sand.

But in spite of the hazards of travel in those days we usually arrived
at our destination about sundown. The tall martin gourds first came
into view and they looked like dark bells ringing against the winter
sunset. We then had to pass some Negro cabins on the farm where shy,
grinning darkies—Mama always called them darkies as a title of respect—waved hearty greetings to us. Sometimes the girls' wooly hair
was being braided with light-colored string, which looked as if it may
have blown from the loose cotton piled high on some of the porches.
At last we could see the smoke curling from the tall chimneys at each
end of the long two-story house, typical of many homes in Dutch Fork.
When we finally arrived I hurried up the steps of the porch that ran
the entire length of the house. As I was lifted into the arms of my
loving kin I could see the welcome light of the fires in the big fire-
places through the glass panels on each side of the solid front door.

Grandma loved to decorate for Christmas. Her decorations consisted
mostly of holly and some red paper folding bells she had kept over the
years. Holly was put in profusion behind the pictures and clocks and
in vases at each end of the long mantel. Even the tall tree cut from the
farm and standing in a corner of the parlor was holly covered with red
berries.

Grandma and Grandpa were the parents of eight living children,
most of whom were married with children of their own, so there was
no scarcity of aunts, uncles and cousins during the holidays.

Food never seemed to be a problem, for the big, dark smokehouse was filled with hams, shoulders, yards of stuffed sausage, sides of meat, bags of home-dried peaches and apples, shelves of canned vegetables and fruits, preserves, jellies and pickles. There were crocks of lard, sauerkraut and pans of milk and cream—a veritable supermarket with no cashier. The barrel of flour and the one hundred pounds of sugar were the only "store-bought" items in the smokehouse.

The Christmas gobbler was prepared when we arrived, but other fowls were safe in the coop ready for the ax when the need for them arose, and arise it would.

The safe (cupboard) in the "stoveroom," as the kitchen was called, and the shelves in the pantry seemed to sag under the weight of pies— dried-fruit pies, canned blackberry pies, egg custard and lemon pies. The sideboard in the dining room was covered with cakes—black fruit-cake, pound cake, Lady Baltimore cake, and just 1–2–3–4 recipe layer cake with chocolate, coconut and lemon fillings.

Grandma never seemed to get ruffled. I often marvel at how she managed with one faithful servant, Duck, and Duck's young daughter Coot, and old Aunt Liza to help in emergencies. Anyway, with bread-making, butter-churning and the care of milk, cooking on a wood stove, cleaning and filling of kerosene lamps, soap-making and outdoor plumbing—to mention a few of the inconveniences of Grandma's day, she always had time to sit down after dinner, the noontime meal, and rock the hours away with her family and her company. Visitors came and went with their children and their trunks, but Grandma always appeared a calm and gracious hostess.

Grandma would have been a dilemma to the modern psychiatrist. She was a child during the War Between the States, and she remembered very vividly when some of Sherman's bummers came to her father's house, which is still standing. They burned the gin house with all their cotton and flax, and would have burned the home but Great-Grand-father was a Mason and so was the leader of Sherman's men, and he spared the house. But some of the soldiers cursed and frightened the family and slaves and took most of their food and horses. Grandma never forgot her older brother Adam's body arriving home from the Battle of the Wilderness where he was mortally wounded. She always remembered her parents weeping and wringing their hands over his coffin before it was buried in the family graveyard in sight of the home. She lived through three wars, bore nine children and lost two. She reached the age of more than fourscore years and ten but, in spite of her traumatic experiences, she never lost her sanity or serenity.

We usually arrived for the holidays on Christmas Eve and after supper we sat around the large open fire. As neighbors and more kin came the circle of chairs around the fire grew larger. The children were sent to other rooms to play, with the admonition not to catch "afire." Most of the time we played William Tremble Toe or Club Fist, or the girls would cut out paper dolls from magazines which had been saved for us since our summer visit.

The news and gossip of the community since summer vacation were the main topics of conversation for the grownups. If the discussion grew too lively an eavesdropping or inquiring child was likely to ask, "Who, Mama?" "Who, Aunt Mattie?"

The old wooden telephone on the wall was sure to ring, and while Grandma's ring was one long and three shorts, it was not considered bad etiquette to listen in on anyone's ring. Sometimes the party line would get so heavy with listeners that parties talking could not hear each other, and the listeners were kindly asked to hang up so the conversants could hear. They readily complied with the request and no feelings were hurt.

After the local visitors had gone Grandpa would get the Bible from the table by his chair at the window and read the Christmas story from the Gospel of Luke. Next we hung our stockings, and the big mantel in the parlor was filled with long and short black or white stockings. Mama or one of my aunts would play "Silent Night," or "Away in a Manger," on the old reed organ—later the piano—and all would gather around and sing the tender familiar carols. Then it was time for the children to go to bed so that Santa Claus could come, but before we went we would put a cake, a pie, or some fruit on the table for tired Santa to eat.

When I slipped between the icy sheets I wondered if morning would ever come, but, after sinking into the soft depths of a feather bed and covering myself with a pile of patchwork quilts, visions of sugar plums had little time to dance through my head for almost instantly I was asleep, and in a flash it was morning.

Children came bounding out of beds upstairs and down, but before we could go into the parlor we had to go into the dining room and pretend to eat breakfast. I remember trying to choke down the country ham or sausage and eggs, the hot biscuits, grits, fig preserves and a glass of milk heavy with cream. But it was no use; I simply could not eat, so great was my excitement, and finally I was allowed to go into the parlor.

There was the Christmas tree, lighted with small, real, twisted candles in holders clipped onto the tree. Many of the toys were on the tree, too. There were drums, horns, balls and dolls—dolls standing in boxes, and how lovely they looked to me. Mama always hand-dressed the dolls that Santa Claus brought me, but to my childish eyes the dolls in the boxes with their stiff, fancy, flimsy dresses and turned-back hats were far more beautiful than those Mama had spent hours dressing.

Our stockings were filled with oranges, apples, tangerines, nuts and raisins, with a small gift, like a harmonica for the girls and a cap pistol for the boys, stuffed down in the toe. After the gifts were distributed, the children scattered in small groups to play and to swap toys. Some tragedy like the falling in of a doll's eyes, a broken locket chain, or a burned finger from a cap pistol was sure to happen, but was soon forgotten.

There were sillabub and homemade blackberry wine for the grown-ups, with more company coming and going. The bountiful dinner was the main event of the day, and visiting continued long after the sun had set.

On Christmas night shovelfuls of ashes from the open fires were carried out into the yard, and Roman candles, sky rockets, sparklers and large firecrackers were lit. Their noise and colored light filled the night sky through the bare trees. If tired children had fallen asleep in the arms of mothers or aunts, or at some secluded spot on the floor, they were sure to arouse for this excitement.

Grandma believed in Old Christmas which is January 6, so her cele-bration of Christmas lasted from Christmas Eve until that date with, of course, lesser degrees of intensity. But she kept "open house" so to speak. Relatives and friends were urged to visit, and though the holly drooped and dried up, and the paper bells became a little more faded, an air of festivity prevailed during that period.

But all that is gone now—my grandparents, my parents, a brother and a sister, and many aunts, uncles and cousins. The dear old house has long been covered by the greedy waters of the lake. But surely it must resound at Christmastide with our love and laughter of long ago for ears not grown too dim to hear.

VERA POLENOVA KISTLER, a native of Czechoslovakia, is now an American citizen and a resident of Darlington, her home since she came to this country. She met Thomas C. Kistler at the close of World War II, when his infantry division liberated her town from German occupation, and later came to the United States as his bride. Though she is a graduate of Coker College and by profession a music teacher in the Darlington public schools, Mrs. Kistler lists her two children as her most important source of occupation. Writing in her adopted language has only recently become her "nocturnal hobby."

The Fish Collector

A man wasn't born yet. It was the age of clever beasts, and Ol' Grizzly was at it again. As soon as he gulped down the last bit of his lunch, off he went to his favorite playground. Though a messy feeder, he was careful to wipe off every speck of blood around his mouth and then wiped his paws on the grass. Walking in an upright position, he suddenly stopped and doubled over in a fit of strangulation. He spat out a long, sharp bone and swore.

"One wouldn't have thought that a carp had so many bones," he grumbled as he was walking again toward his destination, the playground. It was actually more than a playground to Ol' Grizzly. An experimental station would probably be a better word for it, since strange experiments had indeed been going on in this part of yet untamed territory. It was a region pocked by several ponds of various sizes, where fish of all species swam back and forth, each kind in a pond to themselves. There was the eel pond, the bass pond, the carp pond, and many others. Outside of this distinguishing feature and the size of each pond, everything else appeared to be identical. Each was protected by a strong band of iron so that no foreign matter could get in or a fish swim out and die in the hostile world outside of the pond. Three times a day they were fed the same food by Ol' Grizzly, and when in good mood, he told them the same bedtime story. He only knew that one, and though all the fish knew it word by word, they didn't dare to ask him for another one for fear of provoking his violent temper. After all, didn't he look after them, feed them, even try to educate them? This last step was certainly the most daring of all his experiments with fish.

Every morning he made rounds of the ponds and recorded the progress of each in his large, dirty ledger. Supporting himself on his huge paws on each side of the pond, he would kneel over it and summon all the fish to the surface by merely casting his great shadow across the water. He had them so well trained, that no sooner had his shadow appeared than their little heads began to assemble in various designs that he taught them as soon as he found them sufficiently intelligent for such training. They already knew the dove formation and now they were drilling the star design, which was by far the most difficult they ever tried to form. Somehow, it always came out as a jagged oval, or a triangle, but never as a five-pointed star as he showed them over and over. Nevertheless, their assembly was always prompt and humble, which to some extent assuaged Ol' Grizzly's anger at their stupidity. Actually, their promptness was largely inspired by fear of being fished out by his clumsy paw which left the victim bruised for days. At times, different members of the assorted fish communities just disappeared without so much as leaving a trace. It became a custom to think of these as deserters. At least, this was the least disturbing way of remembering them.

The daily schedule in each pond never varied. After the assembly, Ol' Grizzly scattered coarse food over the entire area and then watched them gobble it up. He always made sure that they ate every bit of the meal. All this was part of the newest and most daring experiment.

"Each time you swallow this, you will become more like me," he assured the eager young fish. He didn't waste too much time on the older fish, thinking it was too late to make them completely over, although he made them eat it just the same. Some of the morsels were too big to swallow and they didn't like the taste of it, but they ate because they were hungry, especially the young. Some of the elders, however, merely stored the food in their mouths, and when the great shadow departed from the pond, they swam to the privacy of their quarters and there spat it out.

Time went on and nothing changed in the lives of the fish communities. There was the same morning assembly, feeding, drilling of formations and the same bedtime story. It was a dull, monotonous existence, but since the older fish seemed to have forgotten how they lived before Ol' Grizzly looked after them, and the young didn't have any past to remember, they endured it and some were even happy in their captivity. Some of the older fish remembered the old days quite well, but they kept their memories to themselves. They were usually the ones who pretended to eat the bear food but who secretly were spitting it out and getting thinner and thinner, while the young were eating their share, growing bigger and more bearlike every day.

"Are we really turning into bears?" they asked their unsmiling elders, who seemed to be oblivious to their robust health. Instead, they were mum as usual and passed their time just standing still in the water and staring blankly sideways in a typical carp fashion. The carp pond in particular seemed to have divided itself into those who believed they were changing into bears and those who still considered themselves carp, but were openly afraid to behave as such. Seeing how some of their friends began to hop vertically on their tails and imitate Ol' Grizzly's paws with their fins, they no longer swam themselves, but just stood still so that nobody could tell who they were. It was a time of great distrust in the carp pond, for suddenly it became evident that bears were natural enemies of fish. Sometimes even members of the same family became suspicious of each other, never knowing who was a bear and who was a fish.

Then one day, the young reached their full maturity and Ol' Grizzly ceremoniously pronounced them full grown bears. After all, what else could they be, since they were brought up on bear food, trained by a bear and their minds saturated with nothing but bear thoughts? Yet, strangely enough, there was no open jubilation after Ol' Grizzly's announcement. Instead, a profound hush fell over the star-shaped assembly, which for the first time was tardy and somewhat reluctant in its formation. The five points were so uneven that the design was barely recognizable.

"It must be because they are so touched," concluded Ol' Grizzly, yet not without some of his habitual distrust of the carp. He continued with his inspections as usual, sprinkling the same coarse food over the water and repeating the same bedtime story. Unlike the past when everybody dispersed quickly to his hiding place as soon as his shadow lifted, they now huddled together briefly before separating into families which began to live together again. Soon, one family joined another family, and together they leisurely cruised around the carp pond. Nobody hopped on his tail anymore, and all fins were neatly tucked away. By some strange impulse everybody began to swim again in a fishlike fashion. Every day there was some new, exciting discovery. There was a contagious fascination among all the carp over the perforated gate found at the bottom of their pond.

"Where does it lead to?" demanded the young. They sniffed at the holes, and wondered aloud about the purpose of a long steel pipe just outside the gate. The elders knew that each pond had one but they wouldn't tell the young why for fear that it might get them in trouble. In time, however, they too began to congregate there and together with the young they peered through the little holes in the gate.

"It must lead to some bigger pond, or a lake which supplies us with fresh water," some of the brighter youngsters concluded, determined to get the great puzzle solved.

"Or maybe even to the ocean," one particularly bright carp shouted, remembering suddenly hearing two older fish talk about such a place. Everyone looked at the older fish for some explanation, but they still refused to go into that subject. That very same day, however, after the bear shadow departed and they huddled together by the gate, there was an unusually congenial atmosphere among them. Thoughts like "Are you a fishy bear or a bearlike fish?" were no longer thought. It seemed that they no longer doubted their identity, though no one yet dared to express it aloud. There was a mutual trust between them, and something else that was strange and wonderful to the young, and which the older ones suddenly began to remember. The water was charged with excitement which grew in intensity every day, demanding to be fulfilled.

Then one day, the full realization of it came. Assembled as usual around the gate, they became aware of the morning sun shining brighter than ever before. Its rays like golden sabers were piercing the water, slanting toward where they stood as some messengers of the sun itself, beckoning them to follow. By instinct they all began to silently ascend the great pillar of light to the surface where they beheld a miracle. The brilliant sun transformed the entire pond into a vast sheet of mirror, sparkling there like a giant drop of dew. Everywhere the little creatures looked they were confronted with their own reflections. Even their wet bodies blended in the liquid silver, especially those young whose scales shone the brightest. All at once they saw themselves as they really were and their excited shouts were being heard from everywhere.

"We are carp, we are all beautiful carp, and we were all along. How else could we have lived in the water all this time," they carried on, almost beside themselves. There had never been such merriment in the carp pond. They flapped their fins and splashed in the sunlit water until it resembled a bubbling pot of silver. Some, out of sheer delight, floated on their backs, exposing their white bellies to the smiling sun. Unlike the times when they were cautious not to touch each other, they now took great pleasure in rubbing their smooth bodies against each other.

"Let's go to the gate," someone shouted amid the pandemonium, and though the voice was not strong, everyone heard it and immediately set out in that direction. There was no longer any use to speculate as to what lay beyond the gate or where the pipe led to. By fish instinct they knew. The old carp now vividly described the great body of water where fish of all kinds are free to swim where they please, free to look for their own food and free to choose their own bedtime stories. They remembered aloud the times when there was no gate between them and the ocean and how they swam freely back and forth.

"Then this is really not our home, but our prison," added one young carp quietly while a profound hush fell over the entire community.

"And HE is our jailer," concluded still another, almost in a whisper. All at once they were struck by the realization that it was HE who turned them against each other and caused them so much unhappiness in the past. And all that talk about making bears out of them! How could they've been so gullible, they wondered angrily among themselves. They also recalled the unexplained disappearances of several of their friends whom until now they subconsciously dismissed as deserters. Now their fears were confirmed and they realized that they were never coming back.

"Yes," they concluded sadly. "We are no more than a storehouse to Ol' Grizzly." Furthermore, they saw that they were quite intelligent little creatures and that Ol' Grizzly ruled over them by his sheer size. It was decided that cleverness and caution would be their only means of ever getting out from under his clutches and making it to the open waters. They elected the cleverest carp among them to be their leader in the great escapade. He not only accepted the leadership, but had a ready-made plan for their consideration. Perching himself high on the hinge of the gate where everybody could see him, he began his speech:

"Fellow carp, as you know, there is no way of opening this gate because HE" (they no longer called him by name) "has the only key to it. But we can make this gate go down by giving it a big, common shove every day until it topples down. Since this will take all of our strength, we must preserve it just for this one act and not waste it on unnecessary tasks. Every morning as soon as the inspection is over, we will gather here by the gate and give it one big shove. This will give us all day and night to get over it and regenerate our strength. Above all, we must never give HIM grounds for any suspicion in our endeavor, and therefore we must double our efforts to please HIM. Our task is difficult and it may take a long time, but in united effort it is going to work. It must work. What do you say, my fellow carp?"

Shouts of approval greeted his speech and suggestions were made to give the gate the first push.

"No," cautioned the leader to the excited congregation. "We must rest properly for it and make sure that HE didn't notice anything this morning." The carp realized the wisdom of his words, for indeed they had been noisy in their jubilation. They dispersed to their various family holes around the pond, praising the wisdom of their new leader. That night, when HE came for his usual inspection, the carp assembled with such precision and speed that they themselves marveled over their newly found cleverness. Before, in spite of being frightened into their formations, they could never do it as well as now, when they had a purpose and worked for themselves. The sharpness of the five-pointed star was even exaggerated by five fish heads turned rigidly in that direction.

"How clever," grunted Ol' Grizzly. "Just for that I will tell you your bedtime story twice tonight." But nothing could mar the happiness of the carp anymore. Now that they saw the horizon, they no longer minded swimming the rest of the muddy waters. They even gobbled good-naturedly the food Ol' Grizzly gave them knowing that it was harmless.

The next morning, as soon as the inspection and feeding were over and the shadow departed from the carp pond, there was a great commotion by the gate at the bottom of the pond. Question arose as to who should be first in line for the assault. It was decided that it should be done on rotation system, so that everybody would have sufficient time to recover from the pain of the blow. The young carp insisted that they should form the first line and give the gate its initial blow. Their mothers protested and claimed that the strong carp should test the impact first in order to tell how much pain and damage it would cause to their soft bodies. But the young had their way as usual, and soon the entire carp assembly was ready for the first attack upon the gate. They poised themselves at sufficient distance to gather the maximum speed and ferocity. Their bellies quivered at the thought of crashing into the hard iron, but because they thought as one, they were not afraid. At the swish of the leader's tail they bravely surged forward and crashed in the forbidding metal. As was expected, those on the front line were badly hurt and some even bleeding from their mouths. They were immediately nursed by their mothers who insisted that the young should not have been the first, but nobody listened to them. Only now did they all realize that they didn't have to crash into it with their heads but rather broadside, thus eliminating unnecessary head injuries. After all, our heads are the most powerful weapon we have, they concluded, and vowed to protect them at any cost. In silence they gathered every morning at the gate and gave it another shove. At first, their blows seemed meaningless. Some carp began secretly to doubt that they would ever succeed with their plan, but they never voiced their thoughts aloud, refusing to give up their only hope of getting out of their prison. Day after day they shoved and shoved until they all were bruised and near exhaustion.

Then one day, after another routine blow, a faint rumble was heard. Tired and aching as they were, they gave out a tremendous shout at the sound of that sweet sound. The head carp, reserved fish that he was, was visibly excited. He predicted that from now on it was just a matter of time and of preserving their strength. The carp were so encouraged by their success that they decided to speed up the process by shoving at night too. As soon as the familiar shadow departed, off to the gate they went and shoved. By then the gate groaned and rattled after each assault as if each would be the final one. The closer the carp were to their goal, the more afraid they were of Ol' Grizzly and of being discovered before they had time to accomplish the task. Whenever they came up for inspection and feeding, they huddled closely together so that their bruises would not show. They avoided his huge, bloody eyes and trembled under his hot breath which sent ripples across the pond.

At last, the time came when the leader, choked up with emotion, announced that there was only one big shove between them and the great waters beyond the gate. It was a solemn occasion. The fish congregation stood motionless after the announcement as though they disbelieved their good luck. After a while, however, the young began to swim in circles and carry on just like the day when they saw themselves in the mirror of their pond. The elders were moved too but behaved in a more profound manner. They flapped their fins like seals and huddled together cozily in their newly discovered fellowship. With their eyes open, they dreamed the daring dreams of future and matched them with the dreams of the past. The excitement was almost unbearable.

At last the time came to assemble for the last shove. As so often happened, the young insisted upon being in the front lines, since they wanted to be the first to swim in the ocean. For the last time they arranged their bruised and tired little bodies in the familiar attack formation and waited, full of courage, for the sign of their leaders tail. It was at a reasonable hour since their last feeding and Ol' Grizzly by now would be settled for the night, probably already snoring. Nevertheless, the head carp cautiously surfaced and swam rapidly around the circumference of the pond, looking all around the region for any sign of danger. Nothing but the still, summer wind whispered there. Not hesitating any longer, he headed toward the gate and placing himself in the front line with the young, he powerfully swished his strong, flexible tail.

The gate, like a giant robot, slowly toppled down with eerie, muffled sound. Even before it crashed to the bottom, the great mass of fish swam over it, still continuing in the vehemence of their attack. They swam through the long pipe which was gradually widening and before long they began to see reflections of some powerful light penetrating the waters ahead. Having been accustomed to darkness, the light almost blinded them.

"It's the ocean, it's the ocean," could be heard excitedly from the front lines and echoed from the back. There were only a few more feet to go, and they would plunge into the wide, shimmering sea. The young are already leaving the pipe, but something is dreadfully wrong, because their cries are not the cries of happiness but of pain and terror.

"What is it?" murmured the remaining carp with mounting anxiety in their voices, but not slowing down in their mad pace. Whatever it is, they decide to share it together. Being submerged in the water, they could not see Ol' Grizzly sitting at the end of the pipe with a net in his left paw, catching all the fish he could and chopping madly at the runaways with a sharp, crescent-shaped object. In no time at all the struggle was over. After all, a fish is no match for a bear. Hoisting the heavy net over his shoulder he rinsed the odd knife in the bloody water and waded waist high among the floating heads and white bellies in the direction of the carp pond. There appeared to be no sign of life in the dripping sack, only hundreds of motionless eyes staring in hopeless despair.

There were other big beasts watching the carnage but they didn't want to get involved with Ol' Grizzly for fear that he might lose his ferocious temper and devastate their freshly planted gardens.

Susan's Tree

The naked branches pressing against my window,
(the same through which I prayed last Christmas Eve,)
are mute again, as though they too recall
the horror of that night.
I still can see the freshness of her face
as she stood by me in the package-wrapping line,
clutching a gift selected with great care.
It was for someone special, I could tell.
"No," I protested, "it can't be,
she stood by me a little while ago . . .
There must be some mistake," I carried on
when I heard about the tragedy,
and how she hovered between life and death.
The tree knows how late that night,
with all the accumulated fervency from unsaid prayers
I pleaded with the power above
to spare this life in but its eighteenth spring.
Or was it her mother that I tried to spare,
imagining the depth and horror of her love?
Herself a nurse who coolly witnessed countless
bloody births and deaths like these,
yet helpless when faced with carnage of her own.
Hundreds of pleas like mine went up that night
and the vulnerability of an only child discussed.
Children were tucked in bed with extra kiss
and beheld longer in their sleep . . .

The tree gave me the message
even before I heard it told.
I didn't go to see her cold, broken body
put away to mingle with the soil.
Instead, I sat under her tree,
remembering the freshness of her face
as she stood beside me in the package-wrapping line,
clutching a gift selected with great care.
It was for someone special, I could tell.

JOHN W. POLLARD, a native of the South Carolina Piedmont region, has been a newsboy, textile worker, trade union leader, soldier, construction worker, and mail clerk. Throughout his many trades, he has followed an almost lifetime hobby of creative writing, with two book-length works finished. He has written extensively for radio and television, and his writing has appeared in the Southern edition of *The Federationist* and *The News Review*. Mr. Pollard and his wife, the former Claudia Brooks Patton, live in Spartanburg.

Billy Cocklebur

This comes down from my great-grandfather on my dad's side of the family. It was told to me over thirty years ago by his daughter, who was my grandmother. She was quite a woman, alert and splendid-looking, with that rare kind of penetrating wit which somehow finds a wholesome humor in most of life's complexities. I was one of her favorites and she and I got on well during her visits to my home. She had a wealth of vivid recollections from the Civil War, and when in the mood could eloquently reminisce about them.

Her father and his brother had enlisted together and served in Longstreet's corps under General Fate McLaws. She said they were members of an outfit called the Palmetto Sharpshooters. She had previously told me how her father had borne his slain brother in his arms from the bloody field of Antietam, burying him with his own hands back across the Potomac in the soil of Virginia. Also, she described the terrible plight of the men in Lee's army toward the end of hostilities, when not even undigested corn kernels in animal droppings were overlooked for use as passable human provender.

She recited many accounts of her father from that classic, bitter struggle, some of them sparkling and whimsical against a panorama of tragedy. There is one I shall never forget. It concerned the activities of an unknown, highly pugnacious Confederate soldier in the fighting around Chattanooga. Affectionately referred to only by the nickname Billy Cocklebur, this character's story grew into a sort of legend on both sides during Sherman's tortuous advance from Tennessee to Atlanta.

According to my great-grandfather, the annal of Billy Cocklebur arose in the late summer and fall of 1863. The Confederate cause was in growing despair. On the far south flank of the contesting lines, Vicksburg had just fallen to Grant, while in the East the Army of Virginia had recoiled from Gettysburg with grievous wounds, and at the center massive Union forces were converging for the purpose of cutting the South in half from the Appalachians to the sea.

Greatly outnumbered and with his supply lines seriously threatened, General Bragg evacuated Chattanooga toward Atlanta, preparing to give Rosecrans battle on more favorable terrain along the Chickamauga. With Longstreet's army well on the way from General Lee to reinforce him, Bragg turned and furiously lept upon the invader. The first day's carnage was indecisive, but with the arrival that night of Longstreet the ranks of the Blue and Gray became more evenly matched numerically. The following twenty-four hours swelled and raged into a holocaust, with an incredible toll of 34,000 casualties feeding the maw of American fratricide, making Chickamauga percentage-wise one of the goriest engagements in all military history.

The Union left held tenaciously under General Thomas, but at heart-rending cost Longstreet's men made shambles of their right. My grandmother said her father was in the thickest of this action. Mounting assault after assault up and around Missionary Ridge over the dead and wounded, the Confederates finally carried the issue hand to hand with bayonet, rifle-club and knife, overrunning Rosecrans' headquarters and enveloping the field, with the battered Federals narrowly evading disaster by pulling behind the defense works around Chattanooga.

Shortly following the battle Longstreet's command made a diversionary shift to the Knoxville sector, where my great-grandfather was shot through the leg in an encounter near Loudon. It was there he heard first about Billy Cocklebur. Shipped back through Atlanta for hospitalization, he learned the rest of Billy's story there from a Union officer who had just been wounded and captured in the Battle of Resaca.

After Chickamauga Grant had assumed Union control in Tennessee, bringing up strong reinforcements under Sherman from Mississippi and Hooker from Virginia. Then, through amazing luck, hard contention and a dramatic reversal in the fortunes of war, he was able to snatch victory out of certain defeat, nullifying Chickamauga and driving the Confederates from Missionary Ridge in full retreat.

That is, all Confederates were dislodged except Billy Cocklebur, who then began his legend by continuing his battle alone against the Union for possession of the Ridge. Billy's home was said to be in that neighborhood, for he was as familiar with the Ridge as with his hand. Using all possible vantages of cover and concealment, he ranged over the Ridge with destructive effect on enemy movement in the area. His accuracy with rifle was unerring in daylight hours, and all through both day and night his tireless voice carried out over the countryside in shrill denunciation to the cohorts of Grant and Sherman. These verbal castigations were short and colorfully abusive, always ending with the taunt, "We give you hell at Chickamauga!"

The first half-dozen patrols sent out to dispose of Billy returned with only their numbers depleted by his peripatetic firepower. More and larger patrols were then dispatched with deadly results to the searchers and no Billy. The Ridge was gone over and back again by increased detachments to no avail, with Billy's disturbing vilifications and "We give you hell at Chickamauga!" sounding intermittently from a distance.

Billy was indeed proving his peerless Confederate qualities. He was on the minds of thousands of his enemies, he was forcing the proud Army of the Cumberland to respect his convictions and prowess, and he was single-handedly tearing its morale into shreds. Finally and in desperation, so my grandmother said, no less than a full brigade went after him, scouring every foot of the Ridge from end to end.

They found Billy sound asleep in a tiny side-cave near the mouth of a railroad tunnel in the Ridge. Disarmed, red-eyed from exhaustion and lack of sleep, ragged, dirty, starving and fiercely whiskered, he was

dragged to brigade headquarters and thrown into solitary imprison-
ment under heavy guard. Billy slept the clock around and became the
cynosure of half the Union army. Upon awakening and being fed, he
promptly continued his harsh verbal harrassment of the foe. Through
apertures in the stockade he espied a cluster of ranking officers con-
ferring nearby and sent his maledictions in their direction.

"Now, you hear me, Yankee officers," he trumpeted keenly, "and
hear me good all you damned blue-bellies! Where would you be right
now without hard-headed old Pap Thomas? You'd either be our prisoners or buried 'tween here and Chattanooga! Yes, by God, that's the truth
and you know it! If I'd only had a couple more good boys with me on
the Ridge, things still would've been much different! It took a whole
new Yankee army just to put us off the Ridge, but don't you ever, ever
forget that we give you hell at Chickamauga!"

A corps staff officer separated from the group being directly ha-
rangued summoned the sergeant in charge of Billy's guard.

"Take your detail," he ordered in a loud angry voice, "and shoot
that damned Reb immediately!"

The sergeant quickly gathered his men and they unceremoniously
hauled Billy out of confinement, binding his arms behind him around
a small pine tree next to the palisade.

"I heard you cowards murdered prisoners, and this proves it!" he
yelled. Pale-faced and silent, the squad aligned itself before him with
rifles at ground.

"Just a minute," interrupted the staff officer, raising his arm as the
rifles were leveled toward the hapless Confederate, "I want the general
to witness this execution. He'll return from Bridgeport in a few hours
and will enjoy seeing the extermination of this Rebel mad dog. Return
the spy to stockade and stay prepared to kill him on short notice, as
the general's time is most limited."

"Mad dog and spy, indeed," snorted Billy as they unbound him. "I'm
one of those mad dogs that give you hell at Chickamauga!"

That night the guard advised Billy he was to be shot the following
sunrise as a spy. Told he would be allowed what he wanted for his
final meal, Billy requested fried chicken and a jug of whiskey, which
was brought him. Toward midnight, when Billy was mellow with a

full meal and liquor, a man in civilian garb entered the guardhouse and talked with him privately for several hours. My great-grandfather said the visitor was Pinkerton's top agent in the South. He finally talked Billy into an agreement whereby Billy's life would be spared, and he would be deeded a homestead and farm on government land in the Midwest, as well as sent there within a week to take possession, provided Billy would join the Union army and wear its colors for only twelve hours.

A full staff conference of the corps in the area was held early the next day. An adjutant was detailed to this assembly to improve the morale of the men. He pointed out the welcome change in the terrible weather, that their major supply lines were now fully open, and that, most important of all, Billy Cocklebur had actually deserted the Rebel cause and was now a volunteer in the Army of the Cumberland. As he was finishing an aide came through the door with an enlisted man wearing a spanking new uniform. It was Billy, scrubbed, clean, trim of beard, in blue and everything pure spit and polish.

"Here he is, gentlemen," declared the adjutant proudly. "Pass the good news down to all ranks." Turning to the recruit, he asked, "What do you have to say, Billy?"

Already at attention, Billy took three steps forward and saluted smartly with a sharpness in his eyes. "All I can say now, sir," he responded deliberately, "is that *they* really did give *us* hell at Chicka-mauga, didn't they!"

Franklin B. Ashley has published several poems and short stories within the last year, some of which have appeared in *The South Carolina Review, Prairie Poet, United Poet, New Magazine, College English* and in two anthologies, *New Voices in the Wind* and *All Time Favorites in Poetry*. His work will also appear in many other publications in the near future. Mr. Ashley, the leader of a jazz trio in the Columbia area, is currently completing work on his Ph.D. in English at the University of South Carolina.

Shower

The useless using
Of tangerine lipstick,
The warmth
Of cellophane cracking,
The jaded surprise
Of losing to win,
The "sure did appreciate"
"Come back again."

JOHN A. MITCHELL has published work consisting mostly of newspaper features and—under pseudonyms—trade journal and secondary magazine articles. A native of Sumter where his ancestors settled in 1740, he is married to the former Audrey McClary, a Williamsburg County native, and is the father of four children. He has been in newspaper work for twenty years and at the present is copy desk chief for *The State*.

Three Cinquains

This is
For you alone:
Happiness is sipping
The stars while thirstily counting
Cold beer.

***

Love-struck
Flower children
Groping toward the stars
Mill in ecstatic delirium, then
Turn off.

***

Somewhere
A nightbird sings.
The dawn creeps softly in.
Too soon the plaintive melody
Is gone.

***

LUCAS A. CARPENTER, a native of North Charleston, sent his poems from Vietnam, where he was serving with the United States Armed Forces.

St. Simeon Stylites Comes Down

Embracing the stone pole with both arms,
he slides like a fireman down,
beard sizzling and pungent,
until he hits the ground
crumpling up like a rusty tin can stepped on vertically.
Inflating himself once again to the desired size,
he shoves his bleeding hands in his pockets
and staggers down the street,
having forgotten how to walk.

Burnie Michelle

He cultivated a megaphone voice
years ago, before the alternative choice
had even occurred to him. Music
was Django, Ruth Etting, or Bix,
and he played and sang not so much to
invoke the shades of a tinsel age
as to make the statements again, in good faith.
But quietly this time,
like turning the radio on at two in the morning.
He said he'd never played New York
but had been in Philadelphia once
where he walked dark streets in a trenchcoat
through mist reflecting streetlamps on black asphalt
to a hotel room with a flashing neon light outside.
Comfortable only in aftermaths,
he destroyed himself with women
so he could spend hours in some barroom drinking
and, maudlin, think of what they had meant to him.
"I know all the old movies," he told me.

Wendy Mattox began writing poetry when she was six years old and has continued "when the mood strikes." "The Wall," written at age seventeen, was her first attempt at free verse. She has been working as an interviewer but plans to return to school soon, where she will major in English.

The Wall

There's a wall over there
Which I cannot climb;
And I can't look over it,
And I can't even go near it—
Because I'm afraid to.

The animals don't go near,
And no grass or trees or anything is beside it;
But I keep looking
Because it fascinates me.

Some people take stones out of it
And build different kinds of bridges with them.
Other people build little houses
And go in and out, and shut the door.

But I can't figure out what to do with the blocks,
Though they are so many and different—

But most of them black and brown and gray—
But so different.
And I'm the only one
Who stands over here—and just looks—
I'm so afraid, alone . . .

PAMELA J. NAGLE is a transplanted Floridian from Sarasota. She is presently a student at Winthrop College, in Rock Hill. Publication of her poems in this anthology marks her debut in print.

One Day

one day
      before
         I was young
    I rode a horse
        led by a man
        who pulled us around
        in a path of sawdust
in a country of grass

and it was green
    and I sat not tall in the saddle
    nor imagining someday circuses
but quiet and comfortable
        when suddenly
        I remember
            the horse stopped
        and sneezed with a stomping hoof
        and suddenly
        I remembered
        I was a long way from the grass

The Poetry of Absolute Thought?

can the poetry of absolute be written?
    ". . . go to him now, he calls you, you can't
       refuse."
i am calling you
there are conclusions to be drawn
there are truths you don't want to handle
there are etchings in your brain that interest me
perhaps you will understand and not ask with
       your words,
but with your eyes
        ". . . i was watching this morning; you got
          on the bus and just
        staggered around as if you were going to sit
          down at each seat,
        but you kept stumbling all the way to the
          back—it makes me sick."
        the spider i thought i killed outside my room
          is still crawling
        and my glasses still keep falling off
        and the world is a various place to live in
        and
i am still dependent on your accidental smiles

GRACE BEACHAM FREEMAN has published more than thirty poems, one hundred articles and short stories, and eight children's plays in literary magazines, anthologies, and national publications such as *Redbook* and *The Saturday Evening Post*. Both poems published here first appeared in *The Saturday Evening Post*. A short collection of her poems is in its fourth printing. She has written several newspaper feature stories, and her column, "At Our House," was internationally syndicated by King Features for more than ten years (1954–1964). She has done specialized writing and editing for six southeastern colleges and universities, including four radio dramas, and was writer of the preschool ETV series, "Education for Four- and Five-Year-Olds." Mrs. Freeman is the wife of Dr. John A. Freeman of Winthrop College, Rock Hill, and the mother of four.

Beach Brawl

Wind was drunk again!
He swore storm oaths at the trembling trees
And hurled stinging sand in the eyes
Of little beach houses crouched on their knees.

Boldly, he flung open the doors
Of modest bath houses and then feeling dry,
He filled his stein with a draught from the sea
And blew white foam to the sky!

Cornfield

Cornstalk soldiers in shiny green armor
Standing at attention while a brawny young farmer
Strides through their ranks, with joy in his walk,
Proud to be dwarfed by the tallest cornstalk!

Cornfield army, ragged in the dusk,
Surrendering to winter the last brown husk,
Tired old soldiers standing at ease,
Sagging at the shoulders, buckling at the knees.

LEE S. MCADEN was born in Charlotte, North Carolina, and raised in Columbia. Her poems have appeared in the Hollins College, Virginia, literary magazine. She and her husband now live in New Haven, Connecticut, where Lee is a teacher.

apricots

o yes
i sit
in a purple chair
girl
of the green eye
lazy hair
o yes
o yes
eating apricots
hatching dreamlets.

barbara
close the window
close the blinds
draw the curtains
and when you leave
don't forget
to take the exit
with you.

alone
i am
and that is all
a smally
bigness

van gogh
would know
would feel
the real
me
see
i sit
a bit
van goghy

in my purple chair
wrapped in lazy hair

o yes
o yes.

professor

it was a tall thin office
        with book-lined walls
        and one small window,
like an educated closet,
small but knowing.

he sat, but hardly sitting,
        for i thought he
        might at any moment
leapt from his chair
to dance.

WILLIAM E. MAHONEY is a newspaperman and native New Englander whose poems have appeared in several magazines such as *National Parks* and a national anthology of pet poems, as well as many newspapers. Author of a small collection of poems, he wrote a column of humorous verse that was syndicated in several East Coast newspapers. He has lived in Columbia for eleven years, is married and has a daughter.

Henry Small

Those who would squander youth for cold rewards
Might best remember wealthy Henry Small:
When young he dreamed of islands and romance
And sailboats in the sun were like a call.

The money first, he thought, and then the dream
And endless years upon some tawny beach;
The money grew and faster came his way
While all the rest grew farther from his reach.

And now with bowl of bread and milk in hands
Grown weaker than those of the racing clock,
He tries to tempt a stomach long-repelled
While spurned romance lies rotting at the dock.

Huckster

Pity the salesman who would sell
Most anything to anyone—
Hawking the Bible to the meek,
And to their enemies a gun.

BETTY RICHARDS FORD had her first poem published in 1965. She is listed in the 1970 edition of *International Who's Who in Poetry* and is a member of the North Carolina Poetry Society. She has poems in several anthologies, *Red Clay Reader II, A Time for Poetry,* and *Poetry of Our Times.* Magazines and newspapers in which her poetry has appeared are: *The American Poet, Graffiti, The Above Ground Review, Bay Leaves, North Carolina Poetry Society Award Winning Poems, Raleigh News and Observer,* and the *Hickory Daily Record.* A winner in numerous poetry contests, she has received two honorable mentions in the *Writer's Digest* International Poetry Competition. In the last year, several of her articles have been published. Mrs. Ford was born in Charleston in 1940. She lived with her parents in Greenville until they moved to Hickory, North Carolina, where she now lives with her two children.

Return

I came from the North
where my children sleep.

Through Lincolnton
>   where my daughter begged to ride home
>   in the trailer with her first pony,
>   where my three-year-old and I
>   won ribbons in a horse show

Into Gastonia
>   where I fell in love
>   with a freckled-faced calf
>   the spring I was ten,
>   where now the Interstate grazes
>   the cow dung of Uncle Dane's dairy

Across the state line

Past McConnells
>   where cousins roamed

152

in a being-remodeled
plantation home
of books in Old English
and a bear skin rug,
we gigged frogs
with a nail in a stick,
where a chained fox cub
ate scraps from my hand
and bit the end from my thumb

Bypass Chester

where my transit home
had twelve-foot ceilings
and yellowing pearl keys
on the grand piano,
we waded in panties and bottoms
in the shallow sand creek,
where peach fuzz, Saturday movies
and slow summer were one

Dried weeds now

where I remember cotton
Pines and brown fields

rolling in monotony South

To Columbia

where I, a foundling,
waited in the Children's Home,
where now I walk to workshops
to readings
to blisters
over USC's campus,
where now James Dickey inspires
midnight sessions
of turkey, ham and cheese
on mustard and rye,
Where we drink wine
flavored by
comrades in conversation

JANE E. SMITH is a Columbian whose ability received early recognition in the *Dreher High School Literary Anthology*. A number of her poems were also selected for the *High School Literary Yearbook*, published by the University of South Carolina. Mrs. Smith was one of the youngest writers selected to attend the 1969 Fiction and Poetry Conference, co-sponsored by the Tricentennial Commission and the University of South Carolina.

H.K.E.

Ironed hair that swings, free, to her hips;
Slender calves in leather boots encased;
Pale brown slicker on her scornful lips
Brows that arch forever in distaste;
She wends her way among the rabbled crowd
That soils her hands, contaminates her air,
As did the masses that to Caesar bowed
And turning, tosses back her heavy hair.
She cannot cast her lot where others will.
She doesn't fit the pattern, or the mold,
And so must live a life apart, and fill
Her deeps of loneliness with dreams of gold.
And with Cassandrian peer at coming years,
Unnoted, damps her bootless bed with tears.

ROBERT W. HILL, presently a Ph.D. candidate at the University of Illinois, has published poems in *The Red Clay Reader, Poem,* and *The Arlington Quarterly.*

Short Ride by An Older Hitch-hiker

Yes, new driver in a red, tach-decked Futura—
(Your engine lopes from cam or tinkering)—
I graduated from East Mecklenburg High School
Before your school was built,
Or your young friend's older sisters ever lusted
For the likes of you.

The Snow Came

During an argument day—
A hopeful belly-flop to skid forever
Forward, but three inches of dry snow
Could not bear such weight and collapsed
Into the sudden breath-hard earth.
Front- and back-porch lights
Lit up the slope that rose high above
The rear of the house and slid away into
Too much dark across a road
Reformed and edged by the deaf white.
One kicked a sweet-stinging white wind across
The playful hider-behind-bushes who
Had sneaked out for fun now to run and
Reckless roll down the backyard slope,
Old cardboard hulks as sledlike failures,
Garbage lids to sling big sprays farther
And wider into the wind.
Glasses of two faces, rough snow, melded
In body heat and the cold wind, solidified
Forever to the lenses, fogged the rest,
Hazed the light spreading in hundred-watt
Joy to the next duplex, faintly touching dark trees across the road,
Hopelessly leaning into other windows
That have held arguments too, but did not
Send two people forth to sweat
With each other in wild conglomerations of Southern clothes.

PAT SHANNON KLEINHANS is a Georgian who now lives in Conway. She teaches in the public schools and is especially interested in innovative techniques of teaching English. After years of experimenting in various writing forms for her own pleasure, Mrs. Kleinhans says it is "a happy accident" that she is published here for the first time.

Slow Thoughts on Quick Pictures

A Poem Interrupted

My window spanned a day as gray as death right up to dark
When suddenly came the yellow, bringing life.
Yellow leaves they were, scattered at first
Then coming together making a circle of light . . .

      We had walked down the aisle following that little circle of light, still half-blinded from the brightness turned to darkness so quickly. Seated next to him I felt comfortable and safe. It was a feeling I'd had before, curled up small against my father, streaking too fast across the choppy lake in a speedboat. Instead of being afraid, I had felt safer than anybody we had left back on shore. Now, with Furman, I didn't care what happened to anyone else in the world, even my parents.

      Furman reached over and took my hand in one smooth move. That's one of the things I had noticed about him at school. He always seemed to do exactly what he intended. I mean, he never seemed to stumble, or bump into things; he never had to swallow before he spoke, like I did.

I was the luckiest girl in the world. Furman White had asked me to the movie and here I was with my hand getting warm in his. Now his other hand reached over and very gently rubbed my bare arm. One, two, three, maybe four slow rubs and then he suddenly took both hands away. I thought he must be teasing so I looked at him and grinned, teasing back.

But Furman wasn't looking at me. He was just looking at the movie and picking his nose. I jerked my eyes back and looked straight ahead and my throat began to get that terrible ache the way it does when somebody hurts me. I almost cried. I wished I were back home with Mother and Daddy.

He reached for my hand again. I was too afraid not to let him have it.

Then they pointed up sharply, stopping for
An instant
Like the swing of a lady's skirt.

I followed Norma Jean Hall and Martha Foster down the hall. They both had it, that swing I had practiced for weeks. You could tell they didn't have to practice. And they both stuck out in back in a nice, rounded plump that made their skirts fit.

Walking home from the bus stop that afternoon I decided not to worry any more about being flat. There was nothing I could do about that. I could practice the walk some more, though. I did it all the way home. Thunk. Thunk. I could almost hear a noise as my bones refused to do what they should. Once I almost panicked because I thought my left hip joint had locked and would not let me swing back to the right. But it did. It scared me though and I decided to walk my old way for a while.

Mother drove up beside me. "Did you hurt yourself today? I thought I saw you limping."

I've given up on being a girl. Sometimes I wish I were back in grammar school where nobody cared how you walked.

The backswing: a ground breeze rolled them
Over and over.
I watched them tumble laughing
Out of sight.

KATHRYN JANE BAIRD'S poems, songs, and prose works have appeared in a variety of literary media, including *The Grade Teacher,* a national publication; a local high school newspaper and magazine; the *Boston Globe,* a daily newspaper; the *Winchester Star,* a Massachusetts local weekly newspaper; the *Conversationalist,* the Converse College newspaper, and periodicals such as *Concept* and the *Converse Journal.* In 1968 and 1969 she was awarded second prize in the Helmus Poetry Contest at Converse College. At the time of this writing Miss Baird is a junior majoring in English at Converse College in Spartanburg.

From Mouseketeers and Circus Boys to Monkees

Hollywood! Think of it—
3000 miles away
In some paper and tinsel studio
There are men who run around
In little boy suits
And act so skillfully
They make
Flesh and blood out of lies;
What vivid imaginations
Their scriptwriters must possess!

Hypocrisy

What is bad
        For the goose
The gander
        Gets away with!

With Apologies to Michael Caine,
Dustin Hoffman and Sponsors of
the Cannes Film Festival

The gateway
To MANHOOD
Is not through
The bedroom door.

HERMAN K. HARRIS, of Health Springs, attended Friendship College in Rock Hill and graduated from Morris College in Sumter. For the past six years he has served as athletic director at Friendship College. He has written over six hundred poems, prayers, and songs. He has also written three unpublished books and is now compiling a new book of poems, "The Rejects." Mr. Harris began writing extensively in 1959, his freshman year at Friendship College, when he became deeply involved in civil rights activities. He participated in the Freedom March of 1961.

White Boy Speaks

I was born good and free.
I was born good and white.
I was born to make the laws of the land
So I formed the mighty Ku Klux Klan, oh man!
I tell my little children,
They tell their little children.
Keep down that old black man!!
Keep down that old black man!!
For we were born good and free!
For we were born good and free!
For we are the rulers of the land;
Formers of that mighty, mighty Ku Klux Klan.
All my white brothers take my hand.
All my white brothers take my hand.
Come on let us rule this mighty land;
With our mighty baby white Ku Klux Klan.

1

A crowd of some thousand people
Had darned their bright-colored clothes,
And jammed themselves into this place
People call the—Barn.
They all had come,
To see, hear, and listen to people,
Like Herbie Mann,
The cat with the big jam.
Thelonius Monk,
A great jazz maker,
But that night he failed us.
Buddy Rich,
A swell man on the drums
For white folks on the run.

2

I didn't dig him,
And it appeared that
No one else did—that had soul.
For he seemed too far remote,
No feeling transpired,
Just too way out.
But the little gal on the piano,
Big time soul singer, Nina Simone,
From somewhere in N.C.,
Made her way slowly to the stage,
Took her seat at the piano.
The crowd grew quiet.
Then Miss Simone
Began to play and sing,
Each song right from the gut.
As Nina blew out her soul
The audience received it like
Gold—They dug her the most

And kept begging for more of
Each song.

3

Even Nina's protest song,
Why THE KING OF LOVE IS DEAD
When that was over
The crowd jumped to their feet
Giving the queen of jazz
The greatest ovation I have ever
Seen. Nina, come back on stage
For a bow.
Nina Simone, a true soul sister,
Kept on pushing.

GAY COTHRAN, from Timmonsville, has recently left the teaching profession and graduate work in order to pursue a literary career. Her poem "March, 1966" won first prize that year in the annual contest sponsored by the Academy of American Poets.

The Cham

—Then you would be like poor ol' Miriam.

—And who is that? Not your Aunt? Oh, I remember now.

—No. She collected postcards. But that's not it. The thing I was telling you is that Miriam was, well, plain fat. And yet we all loved her in a way. One had to; she was so horrible.

—Was she hurt badly? What did he do? He carried on with that woman for years, didn't he? But he did have cancer.

—Does that give him the right to run off to Alaska with his nurse!

—I didn't say that. . . .

—And take her mother. Her mother mind you. Really. With only a year left, too.

—Maybe two.

—It's the same. He had no right.

—Well, it still is funny.

—Martha, sometimes I really think you're peculiar. Miriam eats her heart out. . . .

—She eats all right.

—She's the one who won't live two years.

—But she knew all along, so it's really silly of her.

—Knew what?

—That he played hanky with the nurse.

—What's that got to do with it?

—So there's no need to blame him I'm saying: if she knew all along. Now, is there?

—She will die.

—No, she's already dead, wilted and bloated anyway and that's as good as dead. I won't at any rate attend her second funeral.

—God forgive you for saying that Martha. God forgive you. You are being wicked about Miriam you know.

—Yes, let's change the subject. You may be right.

POSTSCRIPT: Miriam died three months later, not two years or longer. She choked to death while eating rare roast beef at a banquet. She was terribly congested at the time, and it went the wrong way or something. He, the doctor, did not fly in from Alaska for the funeral. However, both Lucile and Martha attended.

March, 1966

You know, I have not seen one really attractive young man,
First for a month, September. Then October, November, December.
January, February, March.
        It's March now. My God! Last week it began.
I saw one and felt like turning my head and skipping backwards;
It was a good feeling. I felt good all the day.
        And the sun is out now, that warm citadel feeling
        Circling in and out, around, about . . .
        Feeling good . . . Warm skin, warm faces
        Warm lips, Warm places . . . And this is
        Good too.
Friday, Saturday, Sunday, Monday, Today. And then there were
Two. Four, Six . . . Me seeing them walk by. If I touched
Those arms, they would feel warm as me I bet, and the blood
Running through them would make my caressing hand move and
Tremble. Delightful.
        Come in March. Welcome.
        Welcome sun and moon.
        I have suffered a long, painful winter.

They Repent for Mary Smith

You probably see them too, don't you?
Sometimes walking, shy things, on
Their way to the show,
Or a Sunday concert at the museum.
They dress often in big flowered dresses,
Wear big hats and many rings—
Smell of strong Lavender. Well perfumed.
A spot of blush on each cheek.
All of them belong to Garden Clubs that can;
The rest, to other things.
There're hundreds of them
Stretching clear cross country—
Hundreds of them,
Thousands.
Lonely women with puzzled eyes.
"Lord, whatever happened?"

But God has not the heart to tell them.
Can these children understand that
Men cringe at the feel of floppy
Quilted breasts,
At leatherlike buttocks?
And does it help that the vanity of these
Men is in peril: They must be fed by full jugs.
They must be, you see.
Else realize they are dying too.
Hundreds of them
Hundreds of thousands.
Lonely women; frightened;
Soaking their teeth overnight;
Breathing uneasy;
Masturbating;
Praying,
Praying,
Praying.
But God has not the heart to tell them.
Be we thankful to God.

ALOUISE D. COPE lives with her two small sons in Spartanburg, where she is employed as secretary to a judge. A native of North Carolina, her love affair with South Carolina began when she moved to Abbeville in 1962, "where the gentleness and dignity that was the Old South was made alive." Today she claims the Palmetto State as her home. She is an accomplished singer and pianist, having performed on stage throughout the state for various clubs and organizations. She has also performed with the Greenwood Little Theater and has directed choirs. Mrs. Cope has been writing since the age of seven. She recently had two poems published in *The South Carolina Review* and is now "actively engaged in the business of receiving rejection slips."

White Wind
for Mark

All day I lay with a fever.
That night the breeze from the south
Began blowing. It parted the curtains
And did nothing more.

It was a dark night.
Only the breeze
Moved,
Parting the curtains.

Toward morning
A fleet of clouds
Drifted in,
Dropping anchor
Outside the window.
I watched them and thought
Of the winds of chance
That blew you
Passing through
And on again.

Nothing moved.

Movement

Sitting. The cat is asleep on my shoulder.
She likes the softness of my hair.
I have not moved for half an hour.
I am her prisoner.

Everything
Moves
Slowly
Here, in this room.

One is allowed the luxury
Of being a cat's prisoner
Suspended
Here where
Everything
Moves
Slowly.

Walking. There is something appealing,
I think,
About people walking.
Not the way the poor walk,
For they have to,
But in walking just to be
Walking.

Of course those who walk
Probably don't like it.
They had rather ride like me
And say from the distance of the car,
"There is something appealing,
I think,
About people walking."

Running. "It is not good for me to relate to you."

Keep a distance, then,
And let us speak politely in passing.

Keep a calm heart.
Guard it from confusions. This I would wish for you.
But in my room,
Alone,
I meet the other you,
The one who has not been born yet,
And we talk
And make love
And there is no confusion.

Meanwhile, earthbound,
You run for the security of your wife.

Hattie's Rhythm
(from "Songs of the Carolinas")

The other girls don't have what I do.
I know how to bounce my breasts
And toss my hips right and left,
Up and down,
And I feel the men's hot eyes watching
Watching.

I don't let them touch me.
They may only look
And smack their lips.
That's all I'll give them.

The girls watch and whisper
And are jealous
When I walk down the street.

LOUISE HAMMERBECK SELLERS, the wife of a United States Treasury agent, claims moving as her major occupation. She has three school-age children of her own and has taught in the public schools of Minnesota, Florida, and South Carolina. Mrs. Sellers is presently director of the music program at Ebenezer Presbyterian Church, Rock Hill. Her writings have appeared in such national publications as *Modern Maturity*, *Sunday Digest*, *Motor Camping*, *Grade Teacher*, and *Seventeen*.

Christmas Eve at the Hospital

The doctors had come and the doctors had gone,
    sending everybody home they could, but me.
I had a fever.
Somewhere along in the borning, something
    had gone wrong.
There were three empty beds in my room
    and a host of others down the hall.
The nursery was empty save for my
    new little Jon.
Then they wheeled her in, this slender child,
    and placed her on the bed
    across from mine.
Her feet stuck out from underneath the sheets—
    their bottoms very dirty.
She spoke to me, a giggle voice—
    proud she was she hadn't even made it to the labor room
    before the baby came.
But then, this was her second and seconds usually

come earlier, she said, or she'd been told so.
And what was mine? The first!
And I so *old*. (She actually said *old*.)
I had to smile, for I was almost thirty
　　and she was just sixteen.

She was surprised and said so, right aloud to me,
　　that I didn't have any flowers.
She'd kill her man, she said, if he didn't bring her a bunch
　　as big as God Almighty, and new lingerie,
　　and candy, and a lot of other things.
She got them, too. From him,
　　and from her parents.
But she was just sixteen.

I wasn't sad. I was full of the world, inside.
I didn't need to look at it,
　　or have it shown to me.
No, I wanted to tell her, but didn't
　　spoil her brief moment of glee—

I had roses enough when I was sixteen.
All they ever did was die.

MARILYN BETH MAHONEY is a nineteen-year-old student at Rider College in Trenton, New Jersey, which she entered after being educated in Columbia schools. She was the youngest member attending South Carolina's first Poetry Workshop at Columbia in 1967, and her first published poems appeared in the workshop's collection.

To Edna Millay's "Tavern"

I have a friend who has a tavern for
    all gray-eyed people.
And even though my eyes are green,
    I think she'll let me in.
Because once we sat together
    somewhere on a bleak coast,
    warmed hands by a fire,
  And even then, she thought my green eyes gray.